# CREATING A TRANSFORMATIVE CHURCH CULTURE

Martin Leo Jones

Copyright © 2015 Pending
Martin Leo Jones
All rights reserved.
ISBN: 1517530792
ISBN-13:9781517530792

# FOR MY MOTHER AND FATHER

*I could stretch a mile if I did not have to walk back.* My mother was full of these witticisms. I believe my dad actually walked to school twenty miles in the snow – uphill both ways. These are the super heroes that raised me: Leo and Rachael Jones.

Now that I have raised three children myself, I have a greater appreciation for the sacrifices my parents made for me. Like the time they took on the payments for my car so I could go to school or all the times my mother picked me up from school to take me to the doctor after an injury (this seemed to happen often). The removal of wisdom teeth, surgery on both my knees, the setting of a broken nose, and a concussion that I don't even remember are all just a few of the medical costs that never cost me, but I know now it cost them. No wonder they never had a new car or a really nice house (I grew up in a trailer house) until I moved out--they spent all their money on me (or a lot of it). Looking back, I think we never had a lot of money, but when I was a kid, I never noticed it. I ate fresh vegetables from our garden and meat with every meal. I always had good clothes to wear and new shoes for school. I always felt safe, secure, and well-provided for. This is the environment that my parents made for me.

I am thankful for a stay at home mom and a hard working father who taught me the value of home and work. I am thankful for a mother and father that took me to church every Sunday even as a teenager when I did not want to go. I am thankful for the worn out, well-read Bibles lying around the house as I grew up. Finally, as I am writing this book, I am thankful that my 92-year-old father and 84-year-old mother are still with us. Thanks, Mom and Dad, for all you did.

# Table of Contents

For My Mother and Father .................................................................................. iii
Chapter 1: Introduction ....................................................................................... 1
**Section 1: Transformative Culture** ................................................................. 4
Chapter 2: What Is a Transformative Culture? .................................................. 4
Chapter 3: The Transformative Culture: Learning to Listen ............................. 5
Chapter 4: Transformative Culture: A Different Way of Thinking .................. 15
Chapter 5: The Right Ingredients of a Transformative Culture ...................... 23
Chapter 6: The Mantra of a Transformative Culture ...................................... 28
**Section 2: Getting People into the Word** .................................................... 33
Chapter 7: Start with Jesus ................................................................................ 33
Chapter 8: Start Where People Are: Hang Out with Lost People .................. 34
Chapter 9: Limit Your Focus: Start with YOUR People Group ....................... 36
Chapter 10: Go Like Jesus .................................................................................. 38
Chapter 11: Wanted: Receptive People ............................................................ 42
Chapter 12: Characteristics of the Person of Peace ......................................... 44
Chapter 13: Examples of Persons of Peace ....................................................... 47
Chapter 14: Engage the Person of Peace: Proclaim the Nearness of the Kingdom ...... 48
Chapter 15: Overcoming Fear: Prepare to Be Bitten ....................................... 59
Chapter 16: Tools to Help Discover the Person of Peace ................................ 64
**Section 3: Getting the Word into People** ................................................... 73
Chapter 17: Creating a Transformative Covenant ........................................... 73
Chapter 18: Healthy Context to Build Transformative Relationships ............ 78
Chapter 19: Transformative Biblical Model ..................................................... 82
Chapter 20: Hardness of the Heart ................................................................... 84
Chapter 21: Removing Rocks: Addressing Shallowness .................................. 90
Chapter 22: Digging Weeds: Addressing Distractions ..................................... 93
Chapter 23: Transformative Process ................................................................. 97
Chapter 24: What Does the Transformative Process Look Like? ................... 99
**Section 4: Christlikeness: the Christian's Measure of Success** ............... 106
Chapter 25: Defining Spiritual Maturity: The Ideal of Jesus ......................... 106
Chapter 26: Test of Spiritual Maturity: Being Like Jesus .............................. 108
Chapter 27: Motivation for Spiritual Maturity: The Benefits of Christianity .... 109
**Section 5: Maintaining Growth With Integrity** ........................................ 112
Chapter 28: Keep It Personal, Simple, and Original ...................................... 112
Chapter 29: Simple Mantra for Better Focus ................................................. 114
Chapter 31: Simple Fractal for Measuring Success ....................................... 117
Chapter 30: Simple Structure to Organize Things ......................................... 122
Chapter 32: Simple System for Accountability .............................................. 126
Chapter 33: Application to Existing Churches ............................................... 130
Appendix: Transformative Process Questions ............................................... 131

# CHAPTER 1: INTRODUCTION

*Acts 11:19–26 (NIV) 19 Now those who had been scattered by the persecution in connection with Stephen traveled as far as Phoenicia, Cyprus and Antioch, telling the message only to Jews. 20 Some of them, however, men from Cyprus and Cyrene, went to Antioch and began to speak to Greeks also, telling them the good news about the Lord Jesus. 21 The Lord's hand was with them, and a great number of people believed and turned to the Lord. 22 News of this reached the ears of the church at Jerusalem, and they sent Barnabas to Antioch. 23 When he arrived and saw the evidence of the grace of God, he was glad and encouraged them all to remain true to the Lord with all their hearts. 24 He was a good man, full of the Holy Spirit and faith, and a great number of people were brought to the Lord. 25 Then Barnabas went to Tarsus to look for Saul, 26 and when he found him, he brought him to Antioch. So for a whole year Barnabas and Saul met with the church and taught great numbers of people. The disciples were called Christians first at Antioch.*

No Christian in the New Testament ever went or was sent to plant a church; they went to make disciples, and as they made disciples, churches were formed. Churches are the result of disciple making. The disciples scattered by the persecution in Jerusalem did not go to Antioch to plant a church. They went sharing the Good News of Jesus Christ, and as they shared, people believed, and as people believed, a church was birthed. Their message was truth they had personally experienced and were compelled to share. They went to Antioch having both a newfound relationship with God provided through the sacrifice of Christ and having a transformed life experienced through the Spirit of God who raised Jesus to life again. This experience was so powerful that even under threat of death they could not stop proclaiming it to others, making disciples, and starting churches. Churches will always happen where disciples are being made, but disciples may not always be made where churches exist. This is true of many churches today.

> **The depth that Jesus demanded created the breadth the disciples in Acts experienced.**

The organization I work for decided a few years ago to reallocate its resources, with a major emphasis in church planting. This changed my ministry assignment to include catalyzing four churches a year. Although I had heavily endeavored to plant churches in the previous 13 years, averaging about a church a year, I could not see the additional money and resources being there to plant four a year, so I desperately began to research alternative ways. My research led me to read and reread the Gospels and the Book of Acts over and over again. Over time, several ideas began to emerge concerning the first century church. Not only did I realize that church planting was about disciple making, but I also realized that the greatest movement of the church, from Jerusalem to Rome, happened without buildings and budgets. Most of the New Testament is written to the churches and pastors of this movement. This idea freed me and drove me to look closer at the ministry of Jesus as the groundwork for the church of Acts: how the quality of Jesus' ministry laid the foundation for the quantity in the book of Acts. The depth that Jesus demanded created the breadth the disciples in Acts experienced.

As I wrote in my previous book:

*In the New Testament, quality preceded quantity. Acts is the sequel to Luke. If you did not see the first movie, you will probably not fully understand the second. In Luke and the rest of the Gospels, we see Jesus' ministry as foundational to the events of Acts. We also see that Jesus was focused more on the quality of His followers than the quantity. At times, He often seemed to discourage potential recruits. On one occasion, when two individuals presented their resumes and expressed a desire to follow Him, He responded with a job description that seemed to include homelessness and abandonment.*

*I would submit to you that quality precedes quantity—specifically, that the quality of the ministry of Jesus produced the quantity of Pentecost. The Gospels (life and teachings of Christ) were the foundation for Acts. Acts would have not taken place without Luke. Jesus had one who leaned on Him (John), three He took special places (Peter, James, John), twelve He called Apostles, seventy He called disciples, and 120 praying in the upper room who became filled with the Holy Spirit.*

**THEN**.... *3000 who became His followers at Pentecost (Acts 2), 3000-5000 who became followers after the healing of the lame man (Acts 3), and finally the spread of the Gospel throughout Jerusalem, Judea, Samaria, and to the ends of the earth (The Book of Acts)*

The more I read, the more that things like this seemed to surface, and what started as an alternative gradually became a passion for me. This book and the previous one are the accumulation of that study and the passion it produced.

*Creating a Transformative Church Culture* is a response and follow up to all the questions I have been asked by those who have read my first book, *Transformative Church Planting Movement*. Some friends and family were forced or guilted into reading it, while others voluntarily and even enthusiastically read it. But whatever their motivation, it seemed to stimulate considerable conversation and questions about the process so much so that I felt the need to address these issues in a second book. Although this book is more about the "how to's" of transformative church planting, it is also a stand-alone book for any existing church desiring to create a deeper disciple-making process.

I did not write these books to be called a writer, and as you read them, you may agree, thinking, "Yes, this guy is no writer." I wrote to get these ideas out of me in a constructive manner and to challenge potential church planters and pastors with a new way of making disciples and planting churches. This way is not the only way to plant a church, but it is the way that gives me passion. Although I am open to planting a church using any method in which resources are available, this alternative has become more crucial to me. I am driven by a sense of urgency that if we do not have a plan for making disciples that is not so highly dependent on money, we will never get ahead of the increasing curve of lostness in America. If we do not reach into the people of the pews, the laypersons, the parishioners, in such a way that all believers see themselves as disciple makers, Christianity will continue to decline in our nation. Although God's church will never die, the church in America can and is dying from the lack of disciple makers planting churches.

I have often been told by the men and women that I've served that listening to me is like drinking water out of a fire hydrant. It seems that after years of doing this I would have caught on to their glazed look or yawns and shut up, but I'm a slow learner. So, I guess these books come from my need to get these ideas out of me and still keep my friends. Seriously, I would not do this if others did not encourage me to write. My previous book has been met with mixed reviews that range from disinterest to, and I quote, "This is a bullet that fits my gun." Since I published it, I have started mentoring several guys through the process of becoming transformative church planting network leaders. *Creating a Transformative Church Culture*, as I said, is a result of many conversations and questions I had with these individuals and others. It is also a result of the questions asked by existing pastors who felt that many of the principles in my previous book were transferable to their setting.

# SECTION 1: TRANSFORMATIVE CULTURE

## CHAPTER 2: WHAT IS A TRANSFORMATIVE CULTURE?

*John 4:13-14 (NIV) Jesus answered, "Everyone who drinks this water will be thirsty again, 14 but whoever drinks the water I give them will never thirst. Indeed, the water I give them will become in them a spring of water welling up to eternal life."*

What if your next drink of water was the last one you would ever need? What if the last meal you ate was the last one you would ever have to have? Now, I know some people live to eat, while others (like me) eat to live, so this sounds great to me. Self-sustainability, no longer needing to eat or drink, would free up so much of our time. To go places and live your day without any thought of your next meal is freeing. What if the hungry of the world could be given this ability? What if they could receive life, a good life, without the need for food and water? In John 4, Jesus meets a woman at a well on His way through Samaria. This woman lived in the desert and had to go and get water every day just to maintain life. Water to her was life. What Jesus described to her was amazing—a spring within that would meet this great need and eliminate this great burden of having to get water every day. A spring on the inside was far more desirable than a well on the outside. Of course, Jesus was not talking about literal water; He was talking about spiritual water for thirsty souls. A thirsty soul can be just as powerful as a thirsty body. The desire for inner satisfaction, success, and significance can be insatiable. Jesus was describing, on some level, the difference between religion and a true relationship with God. God frees you from the well by giving you a well within. The picture and contrast is amazing. The well must be traveled to while the spring travels with you. The well is deep and requires great effort to draw from while in a spring water comes to you. The spring within changes everything.

> *A transformative culture is a spring within, a water-producing environment that changes one from the inside out.*

A transformative culture is a spring within, a water-producing environment that changes one from the inside out. It is not about something given to you regularly to meet your needs; it is about something produced in you that meets your needs and, once experienced, compels you to help others discover the Living Water. A transformative culture is an environment where transformation happens naturally for the glory of God, for the improvement of the person, and for the benefit of others. It is a matrix through which people pass, making them more like Jesus, who came to serve, not to be served. A transformative culture is a place where the creative hand of God is once again experienced in US for the purpose of bestowing His good work on OTHERS. Ephesians 2:10 reminds us that the purpose of God's work within us is for the good works He has prepared for us to do.

*10 For we are God's workmanship, created in Christ Jesus to do good works, which God prepared in advance for us to do. (Ephesians 2:10 NIV)*

# CHAPTER 3: THE TRANSFORMATIVE CULTURE: LEARNING TO LISTEN

*Matthew 11:15 (NIV) Whoever has ears, let them hear.*

The transformative culture teaches individuals to hear from God, align their lives with His purpose, and teach others to do the same. The great obstacle to God producing a full and meaningful life is our inability and unwillingness to listen. The phrase **Whoever has ears, let them hear** or literally the **The one having ears (imperative command) HEAR!** is used 25 times in the NIV NT, 3 times in Matthew. What a strange saying. It would seem that the person who has ears would naturally hear. It does not make sense to have ears capable of hearing and yet not hear, but we do it all the time.

When I first got married, Karen, my wife would often say, "Don't preach at me. Leave it at work." Later in our marriage, as she began to see and participate with me in pastoral counseling, she amended her request. As she saw me put on my pastoral counseling ears and really listen, she would say to me, "Why don't you bring that ability to listen home with you?" You see I was a hypocrite! In ministry, I was a good listener, the empathetic pastoral counselor, but let me get in my car and drive home, and it was as though I forgot I even had ears. Now understand this: I am a great problem fixer. I can diagnose and prescribe the remedy for just about any household concern in 10 seconds without even listening to much at all. I can name that tune in 10 words or less, so to speak. This is my problem: I just wanted to fix it—I did not want to listen to it. As a minister, I feel I get a good, solid B+ in listening, but as a father and a husband I would give myself a generous C-. Yes, we can have ears and not hear people or God.

Years later, as I began to work on this issue, I made a list of eight ways to be a poor listener and the lies that support them. Karen, my wife, said if anyone could put a list like this together, it would be me.

### How to Be a Poor Listener and the Lies that Support It

1. Keep talking: What I have to say is always more important.
2. Be understood: Always be more interested in being understood than understanding what the other person is saying. If they really understood, they would agree with me.
3. Deny your feelings: I am always rational and feelings never affect what I say or the way I say it.
4. Deny their feelings: Never listen for their feelings because discussions are all about facts and content.
5. Prepare your defense: When you are not talking, be thinking about what you are going to say next.
6. Interrupt frequently: Your insights always trump theirs.
7. Look away: Looking at them may show agreement and cloud the discussion with unimportant non-verbals.
8. Never ask for clarification: If you don't get it the first time, they obviously did not communicate adequately. Of course, if they did not get it, they just weren't listening.

Are you a good listener? When I was a teenager, my mother would often say that God gave us two ears and one mouth so that we would listen twice as much as we speak. Of course, I never really understood it until I had teenagers.

In Matthew 13, Jesus tells The Parable of the Sower. This parable is all about listening to God in such a way that transformation takes place. Using the analogy of a farm, Jesus describes the process that produces transformation and the obstacles that prevent it. Simply put, the seed is the Word of God or the words that come to us from God, and the ground is the heart of a man. Like a farmer, God wants His Word to go on, in, down, up, and out. He wants His words to sink deep enough to produce healthy roots and then grow and produce fruit unencumbered by false and misplaced values. He wants His Word to produce Christ-like character in abundance. In other words, just like a seed planted in good ground, God wants to produce from out of the heart much more than He starts with. While you and I can count the seeds in an apple, only God can count the apples or orchards that one seed can potentially produce. This miracle of transformation can happen only when the ones who have ears to hear really HEAR or really listen.

To be good listeners, we must understand some things about the way God speaks. *What God desires when He speaks*, *What He reveals when He speaks*, and *How He speaks* are all important if we are to be effective listeners and teach others to be effective listeners of God, producing Christ-like character in abundance.

## WHAT DOES GOD DESIRE WHEN HE SPEAKS?

What is God's desired outcome when He speaks to me and through me? Besides what God wants to say to me personally, this is important because it defines the three types of encounters that a Christian should have with others. When I encounter a person and engage them, God is using me to expose them to the GOSPEL, to GROW them up a Christian, or to teach them to GO as a disciple-maker. This is in the context of a transformative culture as God uses us to reveal His Word to others.

### *Gospel*

When God speaks to lost person, He wants them to be saved. Sometimes my encounters with a person are about exposing them to the Gospel, helping them to hear the good news of Jesus Christ and leading them to surrender to a relationship with God. If they do not personally know God, God wants to communicate His desire for them—to establish a relationship with them that gives them eternal life to come and starts the process of meaningful life here on earth.

### *Grow*

When God speaks to a believer, He wants them to grow in their faith. Like an earthly father desires for his children, God wants an intimate relationship with His children. He wants to hang out with them and influence their lives in such a way that they become more and more Christ-like. Sometimes God places us into a Christian's life to help them hear from God concerning their next step for growth and maturity.

*Go*

When God speaks to a believer, it is not just about growing—it is about going. It is about calling and purpose. It is about knowing why on earth you are here. God wants to give you the life He created you to have. He wants you to live a life that is the best expression of who He created you to be. He wants you to not just be successful in life; He wants you to be significant; He doesn't want you to just survive;…GOD WANTS YOU TO THRIVE as you fulfill His purposes for you on this earth. My encounters with some believers may be all about mobilizing and deployment, to make them disciple-makers.

## WHAT DOES GOD REVEAL WHEN HE SPEAKS?

Words have purpose. They communicate thoughts and ideas. We call words without purpose babbling. God does not babble when He speaks because His words have purpose, and ignoring them will have consequences. The question is *what is He saying*? When God speaks, He wants to communicate truth about Himself, us, others, and sometimes all three.

God is interested in teaching me about **HIMSELF**. Theology means the study of God and has God as its origin, means, and end. God wants me to know ABOUT Him so that I might KNOW Him. It is all about a relationship with God. Jesus affirms this when He says that the greatest commandment is to "[l]ove the Lord your God with all your heart, soul, and mind" (Matthew 22:37). He adds that all of the Old Testament hinges on this command. If I took a total stranger, stood him before you, and asked you to love him, you would probably say it would be difficult because you do not know him. If I allowed you to spend time with him talking and living with him and then asked you to love him, you would probably say it was easier to love him because you got to know him. Likewise, God has expended an enormous amount of effort so that we might get to know Him. Throughout the whole Old Testament, from creation, to the patriarchs, to the Exodus, to the United Kingdom and the Divided Kingdom, and in the writings from kings, prophets, and priests, God was teaching us to know Him so that we might love Him. In addition, the life, death, burial, and resurrection of Jesus, our Emmanuel ("God with us"), taught us about God so that we might know Him better and love Him more. Even today, when God speaks, it is often to teach us about Himself.

> We are the painting, who can see ourselves only as a painting sees itself, while God is the painter who knows the place and purpose of every brush stroke.

God not only wants me to know about Him, He also wants me to know about **ME**. God wants us to know us. James (James 1:22-25) tells us the Word of God is like a mirror that we look into to see the real person. The older I get, the less I like to look into the mirror since the real me is not as attractive as the imaginary me. Just like the inventor knows his invention, the painter knows his painting, and the potter knows his pottery, God the Creator knows His Creation. God knows you better than you know yourself. We are the painting, who can see ourselves only as a painting sees itself, while God is the painter who knows the place and purpose of every brush stroke. He that formed knows what He has formed better than the form itself. The weaver knows what He has woven together better than the garment itself. God knows the real motive behind every thought and the true feelings behind every word, and He wants to share that information with me. He does this so that I can stop the self-deception and impaired delusions of grandeur and see and know the real me, impaired and fallen, but redeemable through His sacrifice.

God not only wants to teach me about Him and myself; when God speaks, He wants me to know about **OTHERS**—the good, the bad, and the ugly of others. He wants us to know about the fallen nature of humanity in contrast to His redemptive purpose for us. In the same way that God speaks knowledge about Himself so that we might know Him more intimately, He speaks about others so that we might know about them and more personally know them. If we really listened to God as He tells us about others, we would be more prepared and less disappointed in our relationships and thus learn to be as *wise as serpents and harmless as doves* (Mt 10:16).

Finally, we must understand that at times in God's discourse He wants to teach us about all **three**. In light of God's objective truth about Him, me, and others, the trivial vanishes, and we can act on what really matters most. Listening to God and His perspective on life changes the way I see, understand, and act. In many situations, God will use His Word, the Holy Spirit, others, and circumstances to teach me the truth about HIM, others, and me, all at the same time.

## HOW DOES GOD SPEAK TO US?

In what ways does God speak to us? God speaks to us, first and foremost, through the Bible and the Holy Spirit. These two working together will help us understand what He is saying through all other means, such as His moral code within us, His creation, other people, and the situations and circumstances of life.

### *God Speaks Through the Bible*

*2 Timothy 3:16-17 NIV 16 All Scripture is God-breathed and is useful for teaching, rebuking, correcting and training in righteousness, 17 so that the man of God may be thoroughly equipped for every good work.*

The Bible is the authority on our faith and practice. It is our guidebook, our owner's manual; it gives us the specifications and maintenance requirements for our lives. The Bible and what God reveals about Jesus Christ are the most important filters for determining truth. Our intellect, experiences, and traditions should be filtered through God's Word to evaluate them for truth.

Psalm 119:105 says, *Your word is a lamp to my feet and a light for my path (NIV).* Like the landing lights on the airport runway, God's Word keeps us safe and on course in a world of darkness. The Word, like a flashlight, lights the way in front of us showing us the next step, and, like streetlights, it illuminates the way before us.

### *God Speaks Through His Holy Spirit*

*John 15:26 NIV When the Counselor comes, whom I will send to you from the Father, the Spirit of truth who goes out from the Father, he will testify about me.*

*John 16:13 (NIV) But when he, the Spirit of truth, comes, he will guide you into all truth. He will not speak on his own; he will speak only what he hears, and he will tell you what is yet to come.*

*1 Corinthians 2:11-14 (NIV) For who among men knows the thoughts of a man except the man's spirit within him? In the same way, no one knows the thoughts of God except the Spirit of God. 12 We have not received the spirit of the world but the Spirit who is from God, that we may understand what God has freely given us. 13 This is what we speak, not in words taught us by human wisdom but in words taught by the Spirit, expressing spiritual truths in spiritual words. 14 The man without the Spirit does not accept the things that come from the Spirit of God, for they are foolishness to him, and he cannot understand them, because they are spiritually discerned.*

The Holy Spirit is the presence of God indwelling all believers. Just like Jesus was with His disciples to counsel, console, advise, empower, and lead to all truth, the Holy Spirit is with all followers of Jesus. In addition, the Holy Spirit is God sharing with us of His personal Spirit so that we might know, albeit in limited quantities, what God is thinking and what He desires for us in the world.

You possess within you One who can guide you to the reality of all things. As I used to tell my children, truth is what IS, not what you wish, not what you might want, but what IS. Truth is reality. As Christians, we have this presence of God living in us who created, sustains, and knows all reality; He knows what IS—the truth. He knows all objective truth (truth that applies to all people) and all subjective truth (truth that applies to individuals in their individual contexts), and He is interested in leading us in both as we have need.

The Word of God and the Holy Spirit together form the foundation for listening to God. God's Word coupled with the Holy Spirit defines and reveals how He is speaking to me through creation, the remnants of the moral code, others, and circumstances of life. *He who has ears, let him hear. Matthew 13:9*

## God Speaks Through His Creation Around Us

*Romans 1:20 (NIV) For since the creation of the world God's invisible qualities—his eternal power and divine nature—have been clearly seen, being understood from what has been made, so that men are without excuse.*

Where there is design, there must be a designer, where there is form, there must be a "former," where there is structure, there must be an architect and builder, and, I beg to differ with evolution and the idea of random selection, where there is creation, there is a Creator. Just like non-verbals make up the majority of communication between individuals so that actions do speak louder than words, God through His creation speaks to His creatures.

> **God, who makes the rain to fall on the just and the unjust, is doing so to communicate His blessings to those that follow Him (the just) and His mercy to those that reject Him (the unjust).**

Just like the environment that parents create for their children says a lot about the parents, the world that God created for us, even in its fallen state, still has much to say about God. God through His creation is not whispering, nor is He playing hide and seek. No, according to Paul in Romans 1:20 above, God's inner qualities, attributes, or who He is on the inside are *clearly seen* through what He has made on the outside. In addition, they are so *clearly seen* that no human being can ever say, "You did not give me enough information to believe." However, this is not just for the Romans. God today is continually speaking to humanity through His creation. Even today, He is telling us about His attributes and qualities, His power, and His divine nature.

Throughout the Bible are stories of God using His creation to speak to humanity. One of the most dynamic is the story of the Exodus. While God could have transported or beamed His people to the desert or to the Promised Land, He chose to use the method of deliverance to demonstrate His sovereignty. Through this process of deliverance, He spoke to the whole world concerning His nature and supremacy over all. Through plagues, He communicated to the world that the God of the slaves, the God of Abraham, Isaac, and Jacob, and not the so-called gods of Egypt, was in control of nature. One by one, He toppled the illusion of the Egyptian gods saying, "I, not these gods you worship, control the Nile, the frogs, the flies, the cattle, and the sun." While God preserved the firstborn of Israel, He took back the breath that He bestowed on the firstborn of Egypt, including Pharaoh's son, proving to the world that HE, and not Pharaoh, is the God of life and death. God's revelation of His mighty power over creation culminated at the Red Sea where He stacked water for the children of Israel to cross through and then released it on Pharaoh and his army, bringing the greatest power on earth to its knees. God, who makes the rain to fall on the just and the unjust, is doing so to communicate His blessings to those that follow Him (the just) and His mercy to those that reject Him (the unjust). As we engage God's Word illuminated by His Spirit, we understand how He speaks to us through His creation.

## *God Speaks Through the Moral Code Within Us*

*Genesis 1:27 (NIV) So God created man in his own image, in the image of God he created him; male and female he created them.*

*Genesis 9:6 (NIV) "Whoever sheds the blood of man, by man shall his blood be shed; for in the image of God has God made man.*

*Genesis 20:4-6 (NIV) 4 Now Abimelech had not gone near her, so he said, "Lord, will you destroy an innocent nation? 5 Did he not say to me, 'She is my sister,' and didn't she also say, 'He is my brother'? I have done this with a clear conscience and clean hands." 6 Then God said to him in the dream, "Yes, I know you did this with a clear conscience, and so I have kept you from sinning against me. That is why I did not let you touch her.*

We are not amoral beings. By nature, we know what is right and wrong because we were created in the image of God. Our conscience is the remnant of God's creation within us and is our moral center. It is easily abused and easily overcome by our sinful nature and sinful choices. While some may say that this image and the moral code that is inherent in it were destroyed in the fall of man, I would submit to you that it was not destroyed. While at times it may even be unrecognizable and absent from evil people, it seems to be somewhat active in others. Many religious people want to do what is right according to the law of God and may have some degree of success with it, but they are still imperfect and, thus, cannot have a relationship with a perfect God. They cannot truly fulfill the commands of God without being rightly related to Him through the forgiveness that Christ's sacrifice has provided.

*Romans 1:18–32 (NIV) The wrath of God is being revealed from heaven against all the godlessness and wickedness of men who suppress the truth by their wickedness, 19 since what may be known about God is plain to them, because God has made it plain to them. 20 For since the creation of the world God's invisible qualities—his eternal power and divine nature—have been clearly seen, being understood from what has been made, so that men are without excuse. 21 For although they knew God, they neither glorified him as God nor gave thanks to him, but their thinking became futile and their foolish hearts were darkened. 22 Although they claimed to be wise, they became fools 23 and exchanged the glory of the immortal God for images made to look like mortal man and birds and animals and reptiles. 24 Therefore God gave them over in the sinful desires of their hearts to sexual impurity for the degrading of their bodies with one another. 25 They exchanged the truth of God for a lie, and worshiped and served created things rather than the Creator—who is forever praised. Amen.*

In this first chapter of Romans, we see that idolatry takes place when people become satisfied with attributing creation to the creature. This attribution is inexcusable and brings with it God's wrath. Although it describes the potential of all humanity, it does not describe the reality of all men. Some are satisfied exchanging God's glory revealed in creation for idols made of human hands while others are not. Just as there are the satisfied, there are also the dissatisfied. This is not to say that the dissatisfied know God, for they don't; they are just not satisfied with creatures creating creation. Although they may not know what or where they come from, they know that whatever has created them must be bigger than that which is created or anything they can create. This is not just true of physical creation; it is also true about the nature of the inner man. The man who loves his wife and children, helps his neighbor, and does good things, even though he is fallen, also knows that in some way these qualities of goodness are reflections of the creative forces that made him. The remnants of morality and goodness, although not sufficient to save, are indicators of God and ways that God still speaks to His creation.

*Romans 2:13-16 (NIV) For it is not those who hear the law who are righteous in God's sight, but it is those who obey the law who will be declared righteous. 14 (Indeed, when Gentiles, who do not have the law, do by nature things required by the law, they are a law for themselves, even though they do not have the law. 15 They show that the requirements of the law are written on their hearts, their consciences also bearing witness, and their thoughts sometimes accusing them and at other times even defending them.)*

God's Word articulates and helps me to understand the moral code within me. The Ten Commandments (Exodus 20:3-17) and The Book of The Covenant (Exodus 20-21) are expressions of God's moral code. Through these passages, God affirms the right and wrong behaviors that He built into His creation. Through the law, He affirms what by nature is known—how we should behave toward Him, toward others, and even toward self. In addition to this, the law of God also shows us where we have failed in the moral code. While we may experience guilt and shame when we violate the moral code within us, it is the law that helps us pinpoint the nature of our wrongs and understand the origin of our guilt.

Although this moral code can be easily abused and diminished by our sinful nature and the influences of a fallen world, it is there, albeit in a still, small voice, reminding us that God, our Creator, exists and His image must reclaim us.

## GOD SPEAKS THROUGH OTHERS

Sometimes God speaks directly to us through others, and He does this through divine contacts. A divine contact is a specific person for a specific occasion that God uses to give me the next step in my Christian journey. Like an appointment on a calendar, God sets in place people at His appointed time to advise and counsel, often punctuating life-changing decisions. An example of this is the calling of Paul by way of Ananias.

*Acts 22:12-15 (NIV) "A man named Ananias came to see me. He was a devout observer of the law and highly respected by all the Jews living there. 13 He stood beside me and said, 'Brother Saul, receive your sight!' And at that very moment I was able to see him. 14 "Then he said: 'The God of our fathers has chosen you to know his will and to see the Righteous One and to hear words from his mouth. 15 You will be his witness to all men of what you have seen and heard.*

Just as Ananias spoke directly to Paul, God may be using someone to speak directly to you. We know that if He does, it will be consistent with His Word. I am surprised at how often people fall for so-called prophets who say they speak the Word of God but actually speak words that are directly contrary to the nature and character of God as He has revealed in the Bible. Experiential theology, prophetic utterances, and extra-biblical revelation, in this order, are the foundation of cultism. The point is that knowing God's Word affirms divine contacts and warns of false diviners.

For the last 14 years, I have been in a ministry that I feel has been the best expression of who God created me to be. It was not even on my radar until Doyle Braden, my mentor and former Associational Missionary (regional leader), asked me what I would do with my life if God gave me a million dollars. After hearing my heart's passion, he said, "Sounds to me like God may be calling you to be an Associational Missionary." This divine contact and counsel open the door for me to consider a new ministry assignment.

Although Doyle was a close friend, some divine contacts may be total strangers. God, who used an ass to speak to Balaam, can use the donkeys (wife's edit) of our lives to speak to us. But, however it is spoken, whoever is speaking, and whatever is said, it must be measured against the Word of God.

Many times God is speaking to us indirectly through the relationships of our lives. These relationships that God created are commentaries to help us hear from God. The impulses and feelings that God created within us in the context of family can shed light on what He may be saying to us. Jesus often used the natural instincts of family, such as those of parents toward their children, to help us understand God's desires for us. An example of this is found in the Sermon on the Mount.

*Matthew 7:9-12 (NIV) "Which of you, if his son asks for bread, will give him a stone? 10 Or if he asks for a fish, will give him a snake? 11 If you, then, though you are evil, know how to give good gifts to your children, how much more will your Father in heaven give good gifts to those who ask him! 12 So in everything, do to others what you would have them do to you, for this sums up the Law and the Prophets.*

The dynamics of relationships, such as in family, at church, and at work, may be ways that God speaks to me. God can use my encounters with family, friends, and, sometimes, even foes to speak to me. This is God speaking through people and circumstances. In the above passage, we see this. Jesus is asking these fathers to draw from their experiences as fathers in order to understand, albeit in part, God's love for them. This is often the case as God uses the natural affections of earthly relationships to reflect our relationship with Him.

I am not talking about your family being a cliché for teaching the Bible. This is more than a quaint illustration. Jesus is using a real-life experience His followers could truly relate to. Jesus is saying, "Do you know the depths of your love and the height of your care for your child? HOW MUCH MORE will your Father in heaven love and care for you?" He is not just saying we should know it or understand it like God; He is saying we should feel it and experience it like God.

Our human relationships on this earth, at least the healthy ones, are reflections of the relationship that God desires with us. This is why the number one word used in the New Testament to describe God's relationship with humanity is "father." The Bible even says that we can call God "Abba Father" (Romans 18:5, Galatians 4:6), which was the most common word for "father" in the Aramaic language, with an equivalent meaning of "daddy." Again, God draws on the human relationship that He created and a word we can relate to, "daddy," and challenges us to feel and experience the fatherhood of God. Twice in my life, I have had the opportunity to understand the love of my heavenly father. As a son, I had a father who loved me and provided for my needs, and as father myself, I understand the sacrificial love of God toward me as I know I would lay down my life for each of my children. Even though these experiences of God's design show me a lot about God, my fatherhood, and all it entails, it pales in comparison to the reality of the love of my Heavenly Father—*how much **more** will your Father in heaven give good gifts to those who ask him!*

Again, the Bible forms the guide or matrix by which we understand relationships. Thus, it is important to know the Bible in order to hear how God is speaking to us.

## GOD SPEAKS THROUGH THE CIRCUMSTANCES OF LIFE

How many of us would agree that God uses situations and circumstance to speak to us? God's Word helps us perceive what He is communicating through these circumstances. Let's face it. The Bible is full of God working with men and women through the circumstances of life.

In the Old Testament, God spoke to His people through the Babylonian Captivity. In the book of Judges, didn't God use the pagan people around Israel to remind them they were wandering away from Him? We see several examples of God using circumstances to speak to His people, including speaking to Jeremiah, Hosea, and Jonah. In Jeremiah 18, God tells Jeremiah to go to the potter's house and uses the everyday activities of the potter to teach Jeremiah a lesson about the sovereignty of God as God prepares him to warn Israel of coming judgment. The book of Hosea uses the context of marriage and family to teach about

God's enduring love and mercy to an adulterous people.

In the story of Jonah, God uses a storm, a big fish, a tree, and a worm, all to attempt to teach Jonah about His mercy. One lesson we can learn from these circumstances is God's sovereignty over a reluctant prophet. Jonah is a prime example of obedience without honor, for although Jonah did what God told him to do, he did not like it, and even at one point, he expressed his disgust with God's character and nature. God used these experiences to show Jonah His great mercy that surpassed Jonah's hatred, but Jonah never got it. Although Jonah wanted God's love and compassion for him and his people, he was angry at God when He showed these same qualities to his enemies. Jonah stands as an example of how God engineers circumstances to teach His people.

> It stumped me for a time, but then as I read the New Testament, it dawned on me: Jesus was the fulfillment of His religion.

In the Gospels, we see Jesus revealing Himself in the regular observances of the Jewish feasts. It was the Jewish leaders' ignorance of the Old Testament and their refusal to see the feasts as a means to see the Messiah, not as an end in themselves, that caused their rejection of Jesus as the Messiah. I once met a person who was part of a Messianic Christian group, which had as one of its purposes "to return the church to its Jewish roots." On one occasion, the pastor of the church asked me why I would accept Christ yet reject His religion. It stumped me for a time, but then as I read the New Testament, it dawned on me: Jesus was the fulfillment of His religion. When Jesus said He did not come to destroy the law and the prophets but to fulfill them, He was not just talking about His teachings but also His life purpose. He was not just a part of the story, He was the story, while all the Jewish feasts required by God in the Old Testament were foreshadows of Jesus, Himself. In the Jewish Feast of Lights, Jesus said He was the light of the world. In the Passover, He said that He was the Lamb of God. When I worship Jesus, I participate in the reality of every event that God commanded His people to commemorate. These events were situations and planned circumstances to teach His people about Him and His plan of redemption.

The Bible is full of God-ordained situations and circumstances that can prepare us to see, know, understand, and participate in the plan of God. As we read and understand how God orchestrated events in the past to speak to His people, we are better equipped to see and engage this work in our world today.

All of this means that God is ever and always speaking in many ways, just as He has in the past. If you believe that God is all-present, meaning He is everywhere you are; if you believe that He is all-knowing; if you believe that He is all-powerful, meaning He can do whatever He wants; and if you believe that God loves you and wants to have and maintain a relationship with you, THEN you must believe that God is speaking to you and me 24/7. If all of this is true, then God is not limited to my Bible study or Quiet Time. He is not just there when I open my Bible. He is there all the time. He is always, in every part of my life, attempting to teach me spiritual things, things that are so important that they will last for an eternity. A transformative culture is one that teaches others to effectively hear these eternal truths from God, and its effectiveness is measured in doing, not just hearing. In Matthew 7

Jesus ends the Sermon on the Mount with the story of *The Wise and Foolish Builders*, where the only difference between the foolish builder, who builds his house on the sand, and the wise builder, who builds his house on the rock, is application: hearing that leads to doing. Application is the difference between the person who is demolished by the storms of life and the person who triumphs over them. God's revealed truth that requires change in us that we don't allow to change us will instead produce God's judgment on us. **Whoever has ears, let him hear!**

# CHAPTER 4: TRANSFORMATIVE CULTURE: A DIFFERENT WAY OF THINKING

Most missionaries will tell you that moving to a new culture requires a new way of thinking. New cultures, new languages, and new values: all require a different way of thinking in order to be effective in ministry and mission. While performing a wedding with a missionary to China (for his daughter who was a member of my church), I noticed him stumbling over the simplest of English words. Throughout his message, he would look at his daughter, the bride (also raised in China), and say a word in Chinese that she would translate for him into English. I was amazed that this man, raised in America, was struggling with the simplest of words in his native language. Later he explained to me that he had just arrived in the States but was still thinking in the language of his mission field; his brain was still wired for Mandarin Chinese. Different cultures require different ways of thinking and a part of being fluent in another language is the ability to think in that language. In the same way that different cultures require different ways of thinking, a transformative culture involves a different way of thinking. This thinking is not traditional or "rut" thinking. What language are you thinking in?

## THINK CONDUIT NOT CONTAINER

A transformative culture requires thinking of the church as a conduit, not a container. A conduit moves substances such as fluids from one place to another without restriction. A container, on the other hand, hoards a substance. Like a channel that moves water from one place to another, God's desire has always been not just to work IN His people but THROUGH His people. God created Israel to be a conduit, not a container. He did not create a relationship with them so that they might hoard His truth but so that they would spread it throughout the world. God told Abraham that THROUGH his descendants all the nations of the world would be blessed (Genesis 18:18 and 20:18). Of course, the ultimate meaning of this is Jesus Christ, but remember that what God could have done in one generation He chose to do through many generations. God chose to reveal Himself and the relationship He desired with humanity progressively with each generation until the ultimate revelation of Himself in Immanuel – God with us. In addition, God told Israel, *You will be for me a kingdom of priests and a holy nation (Exodus 19:6 NIV)*. As priests, they would serve as mediators and conduits between God and humanity. It was God's desire that this special priestly people would be an example to the world and an avenue to a relationship with Himself.

Paul says that Christians should also be conduits, not containers, as we pass on to others the comfort that God has given to us (2 Corinthians 1:3-4). In 2 Timothy 2:2, Paul tells Timothy to take that which Paul has taught him and teach men who will in turn teach others. Throughout the Bible God affirms those who pass on the things that He has given and condemns those who hoard them. Be it physical, emotional, material, or spiritual things, God gives so we might give. God created humanity to be a conduit, a channel, a means, not an end unto itself.

> *Like the Sea of Galilee, the transformative culture is one that teems with life because Jesus, the Water of Life, flows through it, not just to it.*

The Sea of Galilee teems with life as water flows in from the mountains and out through the Jordan River. Contrast that with the Dead Sea that has little or no life within it because water flows into it but exits only by evaporation. Like the Sea of Galilee, the transformative culture is one that teems with life because Jesus, the Water of Life, flows through it, not just to it.

Besides the conduit and the container, there is also a third category that falls in between the two and describes most churches and many Christians today. It is a reservoir. Unlike a conduit and a container, it holds an element such as water until its level reaches the overflow or spillway. Many Christians and churches are like this. They will overflow or release resources only when all their needs are met. A principle of the reservoir is that the greater the needs of the organization, the deeper the reservoir and the longer the time it takes reach the overflow or spillway. This is why many churches have a hard time starting new churches. They have created such a deep reservoir that it takes every person they reach just to maintain adequate levels of ministry. If this goes on too long, the church will become a container. A transformative culture, on the other hand, exists to release resources into the harvest. This does not mean that novice Christians are placed prematurely in leadership but that all needs are carefully weighed against the need to reproduce.

## THINK TEACHING TO FISH NOT JUST FEEDING FISH

Jesus said, "Follow me and I will make you fishers of men." He did not say follow me and I will make you followers. Jesus saw in these competent fishermen, competent fishers of men. He saw leaders and influencers.

*Give a man a fish; feed him for a day; teach a man to fish; feed him for a lifetime* is an English-language proverb adapted from Anne Isabella Thackeray Ritchie's novel, *Mrs. Dymond* (1885). Giving someone the ability to do something is better than just giving them the thing itself. God has called us to give away not just the truth of God but the ability to get to that truth for oneself, from the source HIMSELF. I would even dare to submit to you that this is the ultimate calling of a Christian: not to just feed but to teach to feed. I would also submit to you that this is the natural progression of all truth, i.e., that truth itself craves its origin or desires its source. This is why when we see that which is profound, the natural question is, "Where did you get this?" In our churches, the natural inquiry into the origin of truth has been supplanted with a false sufficiency that is unnatural to God. It is enough to know it and live by it without discovering its origin. People go to church every Sunday, walking away satisfied with the truth they have been given, but not with an insatiable appetite to know the God of all Truth as God intended.

Allow me to amend this old adage this way: give a man a fish and he will naturally want to know where it comes from. Teach a man to fish, feeding him for a lifetime, and he will teach others to fish and show them the source of all fish.

The problem is we are better at feeding than teaching to feed. Maybe because we just do not know how to teach. We through the work of the Spirit have become fishermen, but we have never investigated how we became fishermen so that we might be more intentional in the lives of others, teaching them to fish. Often, we view the process as so subjective and unique to the individual that it must be caught and cannot be taught. The fallacy is that teaching to fish is a natural gift that cannot be taught or developed; only a few possess it and, therefore, are the feeders of the many.

Or maybe it's because we are selfish, controlling fisherman who get a thrill from people always having to come to us to be fed. We enjoy the attention of being the only fisherman in our community. We do not want to be A fisherman; we want to be THE fisherman. We desire others to depend on us, so we hoard the abilities that we freely acquired.

"If they want to move beyond just eating, we will send them to school" is the pervasive attitude of these controlling fishermen, so they create institutions where people have to pay to be taught to fish and call it Fish University. It is only through this institution that one can attain a degree in Fishology in order to teach others to fish. Enrollment in this degree is carefully controlled. The curriculum includes topics like FSH 101: What Is a Fish?; FSH 201: Nets or Poles, the Great Debate; and FSH 301: Marketing Your Fish to a Beef Eater. Because of the requirements we place on fishing, we control the number of fishermen and teachers of fishermen so that the supply remains low and the demand is great. There is something fishy about this. We have created false obstacles that prevent individual Christians from doing what God has commanded.

A transformative culture sees beyond feeding to the making of spiritual feeders, beyond learners to leaders. Jesus, in His calling of fishermen, did not identify them as just fishermen but as makers of fishermen. In addition, at the end of the Great Commission, the command to "teach them to obey all that I [Jesus] commanded" brings them right back to "[g]o and make disciples." Embedded in every individual disciple of Jesus is the disciple-making gene. Now, just because they have the gene does not mean they are using it; most are not. A transformative culture seeks to activate this latent gene so that it becomes dominant, turning disciples into disciple makers.

## THINK PRODUCER NOT CONSUMER

A transformative culture creates producers, not consumers. The Kingdom of God will not grow without baptisms; everything else is just sheep swapping. In the New Testament, baptism is the first sign of belief and the greatest sign of kingdom expansion. Baptism, not walking the aisle, was the public profession of someone's belief. The apostles recognized believers when they stepped out of the crowd into the water. Jesus

> *Going is the real sign of a real disciple.*

commanded us to go, baptize, and teach—making disciples (Matthew 28:18-20). As we consider this passage, the central command is to make disciples while the other three words describe the process. We cannot make a disciple without going, baptizing, or teaching. But while baptizing is the first expression of faith, observed obedience is the proof a disciple has been made. While baptism is first grade, obedience to all the commands of Christ is graduation leading to our life calling. At the very least, I will know someone is a real disciple, not when they come to church as a result of my going or when they are baptized as a result of my witness, but when they are going as a result of my teaching them to obey all that Jesus has commanded. Going is the real sign of a real disciple. In many churches, we have subtly and gradually turned from the training of disciples as disciple makers to the making of pew potatoes who will stand before the Lord one day with the incompetent testimony, "I was there every time the doors were open." At times, we have unintentionally created a consumer environment where going to church and helping in church is our way of purchasing an indulgence that entitles us to heaven and its benefits.

One gigantic question we need to ask is: What in our society produces the results we are seeing in the church? What produces consumers and not producers? Well, one answer is the entertainment industry. This industry with all its advertising is designed to produces consumers, while education is designed to produce producers. We say "every member a minister" but excuse those who sit and listen for years without any movement toward ministry. While we would criticize any educational institution that did not produce producers, the church seems to see nothing impaired about our ability to produce more consumers than producers.

You pick up this end of the stick, you get that end—cause and effect. But it is also true that I can look at the end of the stick and see the beginning—effect and cause. Churches that produce consumers more than producers and that suffer from a lack of leadership are organized to get what they are getting. Thus, an overabundance of consumers and a lack of leadership (effect) are a result of the organization (cause). Maybe the results speak for themselves.

One fallacy is that we can get people into our churches as consumers and then turn them into producers. Like Dr. Phil, I would ask, "How's that working for you?" The truth is it is not – at least not for most parishes. We seem to be satisfied with the very few that move through our "consumer to producer" process. Even then, these few are often worn out by the work of the few to the many. What you get them with is what you keep them with. If people buy into your organization because of all you give them, they will expect that gift to continue. The only way to have consumers become any form of producers in this environment is from the overflow of resources being poured into them. Even passengers on a cruise ship will hand out candy bars to the native children at a port of call as long as they have plenty of candy bars back aboard ship. Ministry, however, demands that you give more than you have. Like the widow's pennies (Luke 21:1-4), true ministry is giving out of our need, not our abundance. Like the widow's last meal, we must give it away to others trusting God that He will keep our pots full of flour and oil (1 Kings 17).

A transformative culture, then, is a producer-producing culture. From the start, the expectation is that God has a plan for you to be transformed and to transform others who will in turn produce producers.

## THINK RABBINIC NOT CLASSROOM

The transformative culture is more tutorial than classroom. It is about the mastering of knowledge that changes life, not just making the grade. My homeschooled children learned early in their academics that grades don't matter; you will work on until you get it. This mentality made them work harder the first time so that they would not have the repeat it. The transformative culture is rabbinic in its approach to teaching and learning. This is the method that Jesus used to teach and equip His followers. It focuses on life together more than just attendance in church together. It is more dialogical than didactic in that it is more interactive, and it is more interested in what they are learning than what I am teaching. Teaching is on-the-job training more than classroom training. The result is knowledge that penetrates the head, moves into the heart, and is seen in the hands and feet.

## THINK VIRAL

A transformative culture is about individual transformation first, then group transformation—personal transformation that precedes corporate transformation. Its focus is grassroots, bottom up, and one to the masses. Movements begin this way. They seldom start with a big group. Instead, they start with the one and then move the many. A transformative culture is like a virus. Viruses do not start by attacking the entire host; they start with the individual cells of the host. As enough individual cells of the host are infected, the host is affected. A transformative culture starts with and focuses on individuals—the cells of the church. Personal transformation precedes corporate renewal, with depth producing breadth.

## THINK FRUITFULNESS NOT JUST FAITHFULNESS

A transformative culture is where fruitfulness matters. This truth is rooted in the sovereignty of God. God never loses control, He never misses a detail, and nothing escapes His notice. I would submit to you that although He is in control, He is not controlling. He allows free will within the scope of His control. Therefore, all that God does or allows is within His purpose, control, and intent. If we hold to the truth that God is sovereign, we must also believe that God never wastes His time or efforts and that His Word and work will not return void (Isaiah 55:11). They will accomplish His purposes.

Faithfulness always leads to fruitfulness on some level; it is never an end in itself. We do not have faith in God that does not produce something. He never speaks or acts in vain, and our trusting in His speaking and acting is never in vain. The God who works through success will also never waste failure and at times may even orchestrate it to accomplish His purpose. This fruitfulness may be inward as God develops patience and character within the proclaimer, but it is always there.

Fruitfulness can be an indicator for future direction, just as a lack of fruitfulness can be an indicator of the need to change direction. The lack of fruitfulness in ministry should never be excused by a platitude of faithfulness. Instead, a lack of fruitfulness should always drive us to our knees. I have often heard church leaders blame their lack of baptisms on the hardness of the community without considering that this fruitlessness might be because of their unwillingness to change methods and practices.

"Every organization is organized to get what it is getting." "If you keep doing what you're doing, you will get what you're getting." "Insanity is doing the same thing expecting different results." "The thinking that gets you into a problem will not be the thinking that gets you out." These are all phrases that I have used to get a fruitless church unstuck and moving toward fruitfulness. A transformative culture continually looks at what it is getting, the results it is expecting, and the thinking that leads to fruitlessness and will make the sacrifices needed to change. The transformative culture always strives to see the fruitfulness that faithfulness produces.

## THINK GENERATIONALLY NOT BIG FAMILY

A transformative culture thinks generationally beyond the children to the grandchildren. My wife and I are at the age we do not think about a bigger family—we are thinking of grandchildren. This is healthy and good. While most living organisms grow to a point and reproduce, many churches grow and grow and grow without any thought of reproduction. In addition, because healthy reproduction costs time, energy, and money, many churches will not reproduce until they have a surplus of resources.

A transformative culture thinks extended family. Rick Warren said that as the church grows larger, it must grow smaller, meaning the more people in weekend services, the more the church would need to expand its small group ministry. The transformative culture would go one step further by not just creating small groups but teaching them to reproduce themselves. This reproduction is guided by leadership but not controlled by them. Just like parents raise healthy children who then choose when to reproduce, a transformative culture trains small groups (churches) to multiply when the time is right.

Like parents who celebrate the success of parenting when they see their children successfully raising children, the transformative culture sees beyond the child being raised to the grandchildren they will impact. A transformative culture has Jesus as the foundation, and founding leaders are footnotes, not figureheads. Measuring by generations instead of size means that after the third or fourth generation, you will have do some research to find the guy who started it. This in a humbling thought for many of us as pastors and teachers of the church.

## THINK QUALITY BEFORE QUANTITY

A transformative culture is where quality precedes quantity. The Gospels church started before the Acts church. The foundation of Pentecost was the ministry of Jesus. Jesus' bar was always high, and He never appeased others just to make a follower. Jesus' church of twelve apostles and 120 disciples formed the leadership community for 3,000 new believers at Pentecost. They were the infrastructure of the first church. The truth is the infrastructure or number of disciple-makers of the average church could not sustain a growth spurt of more than 15% of their average attendance. In other words, they could not handle the revival or salvations they are praying for. They simply do not have the quality (leadership) to handle the quantity.

I was trained to move from the group to the individual: to reach into my community, gather a crowd, develop a congregation, produce the committed, and deploy the core. The core or leadership community was developed last. More and more, as I have read the Gospels, I see the importance of the one. When Jesus sent the 12 and the 70 out, He told them that as they entered into a town, they were to look for the one, not gather a group. Jesus told them to start by engaging the one—"the person of peace." As I understand the history of revivals and the major movements of God, although they created the crowds that often filled churches, tents, arena, coliseums, and even stadiums, they started with the one, progressed to the few committed to prayer, and then climaxed with the outpouring of the Spirit. As these individuals were transformed through prayer and surrender to God's Word, they naturally and instinctively shared the good news with others, who then responded to it. A transformative culture starts with the quality of a surrendered disciple looking for the one God has prepared who will be a firstfruit of the exponential harvest.

Why would God give individual Christians His Holy Spirit if He did not intend for them, individually, to be the primary tools for transforming the world? Why would He make the heart of man the "Naos" or Holy of Holies if He did not intend for each individual to be a mobile temple where lost humanity could encounter the Living God? The character and nature produced by the Holy Spirit in the life of an individual is the greatest witness of the work of God. It is God's M.O. that He uses transformed individuals to transform individuals, creating the church.

## THINK BATTLESHIP NOT CRUISE SHIP

A transformative culture is more of a battleship than a cruise ship. Some who have read my first book, *Transformative Church Planting Movement,* have said things like, "We have those things in our church." They also say, "We have small groups, Bible study teachers, and men's and women's groups." The difference in thinking, however, is similar to the comparison between a battleship and a cruise ship. Both have beds, a deck, a bow, a stern, a hull, a rudder, passengers, and crew. While there are many similarities, the differences are significant.

> *A transformative culture trains crews and does not entertain passengers*

Notably, cruise ships are built for pleasure while battleships are built for war. While passengers make up most of the people on a cruise ship, the crew makes up most, if not all, of the people on a battleship. It is a rare thing to get on a battleship as a passenger; all the people on a battleship have a job to do. While there are a many similarities, this difference in purpose and individual responsibility is tremendous.

A transformative culture trains crews and does not entertain passengers. People enlist and board to be fighters not lovers, warriors not vacationers. This battleship wars against sin, self, and Satan, the very culture the crew was once a part of. They are the instruments of the invasion of God's kingdom with the battleship cry, "Your Kingdom come. Your will be done on earth as it is in heaven" (Matt. 6:10).

## THINK SIMPLE

I once knew of a church that had a schedule that was so full that committed people spent more of their spare time at the church than at their own homes. When faced with the reality of decline and the need for evangelism and outreach, they added another night to the church schedule for Evangelism Training. The real problem was that all the families who could and would evangelize their neighbors had no time to build relationships with them. While we think the lost may be rejecting Jesus and the Gospel, they may just be rejecting the overwhelming demands of the church that they see on the lives of their Christian neighbors. While we teach salvation by grace, being a Christian in many churches looks like a lot of work, at least to many of the unchurched. A transformative culture removes the pomp and pageantry and the routine and rituals and boils everything down to the simplest common denominator: the bare essentials. Like water, it seeks the least resistant way to transform lives and create productive disciples.

What do we need to DO church? What do people really NEED to be productive followers of Jesus? These are very important questions. The answer might surprise you. Do we need Sunday morning church? Well, NO! Before you hang me as a heretic, allow me to restate the question: "Does every Christian need to participate in a community of believers?" The answer is, yes, but it may not be behind four walls and stained glass, under a steeple, or on Sunday. It may be in a home or at an office or in a restaurant. It may be on an evening of the week. It may be many groups with only a few people. Is the church of 10, 15, 20, or 25 any less the body of Christ than the church of 100 to 1,000? In the first century church, no one ever thought of the church as a building. It was always a gathering of baptized followers of Jesus who met anywhere they could get together. The transformative culture is simple and always asking what the necessities are for making disciples.

## THINK PERSONAL RESPONSIBILITY

Are we creating processes in the church that remove individual responsibility for making disciples? Do we create events that take the load off of individual Christians to be disciple makers? Do most of our members see evangelism as inviting others to church and events at the church? Then they encourage them toward membership classes where they can hear the Gospel and become Christians? Has inviting them to go and be a part of these systems and processes of the church taken the place of an individual's responsibility to be in a discipleship relationship? I have asked many pastors to give me a percentage of their membership engaged in a one-to-one discipleship relationship and found that most say less than 10%. A transformative culture thinks more one-on-one instead of one-to-many, more man-to-man than zone defense. Every follower of Jesus in a transformative culture is expected to be in a discipleship relationship as a follower or leader.

## THINK TRAINING CENTER NOT INFORMATION STATION

In seminary, I was taught about theology, evangelism, preaching, and ministry. Seminary educated and informed me, but the work of ministry trained and equipped me. I experienced the difference between education and training while in Glencoe, GA, during my orientation as an officer in Federal Bureau of Prisons. This training was not just informational; it was practical. We threw each other on the mats in self-defense classes. We shot firearms at targets in firearm classes. In both cases, passing these courses meant showing proficiency in a hand-to-hand struggle and hitting a target. Likewise, the transformative culture is about training more than informing. Although information is a part of it, the goal is to see a proficient use of the information; it is not what you know but what you do that counts. Jesus did things this way with His *I do, you watch, then you do it, and I will watch* approach to ministry.

To sum this section up, a transformative culture expects individuals to develop their own ability to hear from God, to become producers, not consumers, and conduits, not containers, and to teach the next generation to do the same. Anticipating quality that will lead to quantity and fruitfulness that comes from faithfulness, this culture also expects people to come onboard taking on the responsibility of a well-trained crew, not the expectations of passengers.

## CHAPTER 5: THE RIGHT INGREDIENTS OF A TRANSFORMATIVE CULTURE

Karen, my wife, has become quite a cook. One of my favorite meals from Chef KaRen, as I prefer to call her, is Seafood Brodetto. I love her Brodetto and promise it is as good as or better than what we used to enjoy at Olive Garden. But like all good things, the forerunners of this soup were not always met with such enthusiasm. As a matter of fact, the first generation of this Brodetto (then referred to as fish soup) tasted like a mouthful of salt water from an unexpected tide on a beach in Southern California. Salty and fishy does not Brodetto make! While I have always insisted that my children try at least one bite of every new dish, on this occasion and after taking the first sip of this infamous fish soup, I relieved my reluctant children and said, "Let's go to McDonald's." The only thing that would have made this soup worse is if I had attempted to make it. I do not know exactly what transformed the "fish soup" my family gagged over into the "Seafood Brodetto" that my family cannot get enough of, but I do know it has something to do with the right ingredients. The right ingredients make all the difference, and in most foods, substituting one ingredient for another diminishes the taste or can destroy the dish.

Just like a Seafood Brodetto cannot be made without the right ingredients, transformation cannot happen without the right mix. A transformative culture requires the right stuff to produce transformed lives. The ingredients that come together to make up a transformed life are the Word of God, the Holy Spirit, the passionate intuitive discipler, and the hungry disciple.

### GOD'S WORD

*Hebrews 4:12-13 (NIV) For the word of God is alive and active. Sharper than any double-edged sword, it penetrates even to dividing soul and spirit, joints and marrow; it judges the thoughts and attitudes of the heart. 13 Nothing in all creation is hidden from God's sight. Everything is uncovered and laid bare before the eyes of him to whom we must give account.*

*Alive, active, penetrating, dividing, judging, uncovering, and laying bare.* Wow, these are a lot of action verbs, and they are all used to describe God's Word and its effects on the heart and mind of humanity. The Bible is, for Christians, the sourcebook of information about God and humanity. It has God at its center and man as its subject. But it is more -- it is the thoughts of God expressed in words. The same God who thought and spoke the world into existence and gave life to humanity is the One who speaks today through His Word – The Bible. Thus, when the thoughts of God get into the heart of a man, they will either change him or condemn him.

> ... when the thoughts of God get into the heart of a man, they will either change him or condemn him.

The curriculum that transforms is the Word of God. Getting people in the Word is the most important thing the discipler can do. It is through the Word that the Spirit leads to all truth, not just general truth, but, most importantly, the truth that applies to the heart of an individual—not just objective true that applies to all but subjective truth that applies specifically to a person. An example of this is that while all Christians should be ministers (objective truth), we don't all have to be ministers in the same way or setting. While you and I could do ministry on a bar-filled street of New Orleans, it may not be a good idea for a new Christian struggling with alcohol to attempt ministry in this setting (subjective truth). It is important to note that subjective, personal truth will never violate Scripture and is always an application of God's objective truth. In addition, this truth, both objective and subjective, is not just mental assent; it is truth that if ignored will have dire consequences. As the writer of Hebrews affirms, the active, living Word, in conjunction with the Spirit, reveals the thoughts and attitudes behind every action and lays them as naked truth before us and God (Heb. 4:12). Once revealed, this truth must be dealt with.

## HOLY SPIRIT

*John 16:5–15 (NIV) "Now I am going to him who sent me, yet none of you asks me, 'Where are you going?' 6 Because I have said these things, you are filled with grief. 7 But I tell you the truth: It is for your good that I am going away. Unless I go away, the Counselor will not come to you; but if I go, I will send him to you. 8 When he comes, he will convict the world of guilt in regard to sin and righteousness and judgment: 9 in regard to sin, because men do not believe in me; 10 in regard to righteousness, because I am going to the Father, where you can see me no longer; 11 and in regard to judgment, because the prince of this world now stands condemned. 12 "I have much more to say to you, more than you can now bear. 13 But when he, the Spirit of truth, comes, he will guide you into all truth. He will not speak on his own; he will speak only what he hears, and he will tell you what is yet to come. 14 He will bring glory to me by taking from what is mine and making it known to you. 15 All that belongs to the Father is mine. That is why I said the Spirit would take from what is mine and make it known to you.*

The Holy Spirit is the transformer. While the discipler may do much of the externals setting the stage for transformation, real transformation happens internally through the work of the Holy Spirit as He uses the Word to reveal, convict, and empower transformation.

Just like the Spirit prepared Peter for his encounter with Cornelius, prepared Cornelius for his encounter with Peter, and directed the whole encounter between them, He is at work in me, in others, and in an event itself, bringing all together for His purposes.

The Holy Spirit is always at work preparing ME for my encounters with others. Likewise, Jesus was always prepared for every encounter with others. John tells us that Jesus had to go through Samaria, but this was not because there wasn't a better, more preferred, route traveled by Jews who wanted to avoid Samaria (Jn. 4:4). No, He had to go through Samaria because He had a divine appointment. In the same way, we must be continually surrendered to the Holy Spirit to maintain a state of readiness for each day's divine encounters.

The Holy Spirit is always at work preparing PEOPLE for an encounter. John 16:8 tells us that the work of the Holy Spirit in the world is to convict or convince the world of its sin, and of God's righteousness, and of the coming judgment. If you and I agree with this statement, then we must always be ready to respond appropriately to the work of the Holy Spirit in the lives of people as He makes them aware of their wrongdoing, in contrast to God's right doing,

> *He (The Holy Spirit) does not just work in the heart of lost people before we arrive; he works with us when we get there.*

and reveals to them the judgment created by this enormous disparity. In other words, for every step the Holy Spirit leads a person toward spiritual discovery (the Gospel or being a follower of Jesus), development (growth or being a learner of Jesus), and deployment (going or being an influencer for Jesus), I must, by the power of the same Spirit, be ready to take an equal and appropriate step toward them.

In God's plan of redemption, He gives man the privilege of working with Him. We must always remember that the God of the universe does not <u>need</u> us to accomplish His plan, but He does <u>desire</u> for us to and allows us to work with Him. Our primary ally in God's work of redemption is the Holy Spirit. Just like in a dance, we must allow Him to lead, surrendering to His movements in such a way that when the work comes together it looks like one. In God's work of redemption, the Holy Spirit of God takes the lead, but He works in concert with God's Word and our surrendered effort to make transformation take place. Like Newton's law, for every action the Holy Spirit takes in the heart of a person as he is exposed to God's Word, we must react in an equal and appropriate way. As He leads, we follow—this is the dance.

John 16 above tells us that Jesus commissions the Spirit to help us. He does not just work in the heart of lost people before we arrive; He also works with us when we get there. *If I go, I will send Him to you* tells us that Jesus sends the Holy Spirit to work beside us. He is the *paraklētos*, literally, the one who is called beside. It is translated as the mediator, helper, comforter, or the one who is called to one's aid.

Additionally, we learn that the one who works beside us is working in the hearts of humanity exposing, refuting, convicting, and arguing within them, attempting to convince them of their sinful nature and their need for forgiveness and salvation. John describes this work of the Holy Spirit in more detail saying that He will convict or convince us of sin, the ultimate of which is to deny the forgiveness that comes through faith in Jesus Christ. Sin remains because people do not believe. He will convict us of righteousness even when Jesus, the righteous one, is no longer on earth to model a righteous life for us. Finally, the Spirit will convict of judgment because those who refuse to trust in God's provision remain on the side of the condemned criminal known to us as the devil. Simply put, the Spirit will reveal to every person what is wrong, what is right, and what will happen to those who continue in wrongness.

This work of the Holy Spirit is continuous as He is at work in the hearts and minds of others around us, in our home place, work place, and play place, convicting and convincing of sin, righteousness, and judgment. We must be prepared to seize every opportunity to assist as God shows the deficit sin creates that can be filled only through the forgiveness provided through Jesus Christ.

## Passionate Intuitive Discipler

The discipler is the one called to make disciples. It is the call of every Christian to be a disciple who makes disciples. This disciple-making disciple is surrendered completely to the fact that God has called him to be a part of His plan to bring transformation to individuals and the world.

Notice that "intuitive" is a critical component of the discipler. By "intuitive," I mean a discipler who innately sees and responds to the work of the Holy Spirit in the life of another. The best example of this is a reflex or a conditioned response. A reflex is the autonomic or automatic response to a stimulus. For example, when the doctor hits your knee in the right place, you kick automatically. A conditioned response, on the other hand, is the training of an automatic response to a stimulus. The best illustration for this is a trained police or military officer. I have heard many trained officers tell about situations where their "training kicked in," or they will use terminology like "muscle memory." What they are referring to is the hours of training and scenarios that they have been put through that have conditioned them to respond to a situation intuitively. While many professionals such as police, EMTs, and emergency nurses and doctors go through a rigorous training that conditions them to instinctively protect and save lives, most Christians remain untrained and even surprised by opportunities to lead others to spiritual salvation. This automatic sensitivity and response to the spiritual condition of others comes from the training that has moved the discipler from knowledge to character, a process we will address later in the book.

> *While many professionals... go through a rigorous training that conditions them to instinctively protect and save lives, most Christians remain untrained and even surprised by opportunities to lead others to spiritual salvation.*

In addition, passion is essential to being a disciple. The truth is most Christians have not experienced God and His transformational work to a level that we are passionately compelled to share it. The Gospel, meaning Good News, did not get its name just because of its message; it got its name because people experienced it. They discovered a transforming relationship with God as a result of forgiveness that came through Jesus' sacrifice. This Good News they experienced compelled them to share with others.

When was the last time something good happened to you and you went through a 12-week course before sharing it? My wife has often gotten onto me for forgetting to tell her the good news of others, such as a child's birth. I get in double trouble because I have not memorized the details such as weight, length, and number of fingers and toes (ten is preferred). On the other hand, I've had no problem sharing the good news of my own children's birth. In detail, I could share length, weight, time, date, and the weird cone shape of their heads. While I quickly forget to share the good news of others, I have never forgotten and will passionately share the good news, in detail, of things that happen to me. The difference is it happened TO ME. What happens to others just does not evoke the same passion in me as what happens to me. Many, probably most, Christians experience the Gospel like second-hand information; thus, it does not produce the passion God desires.

Most Christians can be trained to share their story of regeneration—that is when they first accepted Christ and were saved. They may even be interested in glorification and last things—the day, either through death or Christ's return, that we will be with God in heaven. What is missing are stories of sanctification—the process by which God transforms us day by day to be more like Christ. Stories about the everyday redemptive acts of God in me are the most relevant connecting points to a lost person. Having experienced them, they can be shared intuitively with passion.

## THE HUNGRY DISCIPLE

As I said, my wife is a great cook and as a result has spoiled my taste buds against fast food and bad cuisine, but like beauty is in the eye of the beholder, "bad" is in the taste buds of the consumer. In my ministry I have eaten at a lot of churches because it is a rule: where Baptists meet, they eat. Many of these churches feed the homeless and the impoverished of their community. I have never found the food in these settings to be very satisfying, not just because of my spoiled taste buds but because I am not hungry. Oh, I have on rare occasions fasted for spiritual or medical reasons and I have felt hungry, but I have never felt the ravenous hunger I have seen on the face of a homeless person diving into a plate of unseasoned potatoes, canned green beans, and processed chicken fingers (or maybe it was fish). I have never felt the need to hoard food for my next meal. Yes, I have never been really hungry. Hungry people are not picky people; they do not eat around the broccoli because it will give them gas or dig out the parts of the casserole they do not like. They do not complain about the taste or talk about how it makes their palate sing or not sing. They eat. They eat all of it. They are driven by their hunger, not just their appetite.

This hunger describes the person engaged in a transformative culture. They are hungry for truth: truth that works and that can improve the human condition, specifically their condition. Spiritual hunger is a deep hunger of the soul. It is not just the hunger of our times. It is an ancient hunger expressed in every generation since the fall of humanity. This hunger desires the answer to the big questions of life: "Why am I here?" "What is the real meaning of my life?" These hungry people do not complain about who serves them or the way they are served. Their focus is on the food of truth. They are just glad to be fed... because they are hungry.

What produces spiritual hunger? While a lack of the food will always produce hunger, sometimes hunger is produced by the wrong kinds of food. Just like many sugary drinks and sweets satisfy only for a little while and produce a hunger that returns with a vengeance, the false teachings of the world can be just as temporary and produce a greater hunger for real truth. While the world continues to give out a steady diet of what it defines as survival, success, and significance, the truth of God revealed in His Word is the only thing that will really satisfy the cravings of a hungry soul. While it is right to help others to survive and while it is good to aid others to become successful in this life, helping a person understand his/her significance is the greatest thing we can do for them. Significance can be found only when our life is invested in the things that matter most, and when we are investing our time and energy in things that matter most, survival and success get redefined and are included. Real significance that comes packaged with survival and success can be had only when a person is rightly connected to the Creator. A hungry disciple craves this connection that produces real significance.

> *Spiritual hunger is produced by the realized disparity between God and man.*

Spiritual hunger is produced by the realized disparity between God and man. Looking back at the words of Jesus concerning the mission of the Spirit, we see that He is here to convince the world of sin, righteousness and judgment. In this is the formula the produces hunger: my sin + God's righteousness = judgment. When the Spirit's work is done, all that is left is an impending sense of judgment, which can lead a person to an overwhelming hunger in the soul. The Gospel is the food for this hunger produced by the realization of judgment. The hungry follower of Jesus feeds on the forgiveness that Jesus' provides through His depth, burial, and resurrection. In addition, he continually hungers for and feeds on the truth Jesus gives through His teaching that deals with sin and that brings real freedom and significance to life.

*John 8:31-36 (NIV) To the Jews who had believed him, Jesus said, "If you hold to my teaching, you are really my disciples. 32 Then you will know the truth, and the truth will set you free." 33 They answered him, "We are Abraham's descendants and have never been slaves of anyone. How can you say that we shall be set free?" 34 Jesus replied, "Very truly I tell you, everyone who sins is a slave to sin. 35 Now a slave has no permanent place in the family, but a son belongs to it forever. 36 So if the Son sets you free, you will be free indeed.*

# CHAPTER 6: THE MANTRA OF A TRANSFORMATIVE CULTURE

*Transformation (discipleship) happens when you get an individual into the Word in such a way that gets the Word into them so that they become like THE WORD – Jesus Christ.*

*Remember the Alamo* was the mantra in the hearts and on the lips of every Texas soldier on the Battlefield of San Jacinto as the Texas army defeated General Santa Anna and the Mexican army. This victory ended the revolution and secured Texas' independence. After the Alamo, this became the rallying cry that created this army and sustained its desire for retribution. In this statement was the recognition of 180 volunteers, including Davy Crockett, Jim Bowie, and William Travis, who gave their lives for the creation of a free Texas.

Mantras can be powerful tools. A mantra is a word or phrase that is repeated often and expresses someone's beliefs and desires. The word actually comes from two words: *man* meaning think and *tra* meaning tool or instrument; thus, it is a thinking tool. Today the word *mantra* is used to describe the meaningless, repeated chanting of other world religions. When I refer to *mantra*, I am referring to a thinking tool—a meaningful statement that is repeated often to keep us focused. This mantra not only defines the desired outcome but also the method for achieving it. It is a mantra of transformation.

The Word of God is at the center this mantra. By the Word, I mean the divinely inspired Word of God—the Bible. It is THE curriculum. The curriculum is not a book about the Bible, a Sunday School quarterly, or sermons containing the Bible, but the Bible. This is not to say that books, quarterlies, and sermons are not helpful, but they are extra-curricular. The core curriculum is getting people into the Bible. This is important because the Bible is inspired, profitable, alive, active, and sharp, capable of transforming the heart of man.

Furthermore, when I refer to THE WORD, I am referring to Jesus Christ who is the measure or standard for being what we call Christian.

## THE BIBLE IS INSPIRED

*2 Timothy 3:14-17 (NIV) But as for you, continue in what you have learned and have become convinced of, because you know those from whom you learned it, 15 and how from infancy you have known the Holy Scriptures, which are able to make you wise for salvation through faith in Christ Jesus. 16 All Scripture is God-breathed and is useful for teaching, rebuking, correcting, and training in righteousness, 17 so that the servant of God may be thoroughly equipped for every good work.*

The Word of God is inspired. It is literally God-breathed. Just like you and I take a deep breath and pass it over our vocal cords to produce intelligible sounds that communicate thoughts, God communicates His thoughts to us through the Bible—HIS Word. If you do not believe this, don't bother to open the Bible. If you do not believe that when you open the Bible that God has spoken and wants to speak to you, don't bother. Don't bother reading any further. Don't bother God, unless you believe and trust that He exists and that He wants to speak to you. You see, without faith it is impossible to hear or please God (Hebrews 11:6). This emphasis on the Bible does not mean that God does not speak in other ways, such as through people, situations, and circumstances. It means, however, that the primary source of our ability to hear and understand *when, where, how,* and *what* is His Word.

## THE BIBLE IS PROFITABLE

The Word of God is profitable, useful. This means that it works. God's Word is not just a good idea—it is the ideal. It is not just theoretical but practical. Do you want to do good, live a good life, be a good person? Then get into God's Word and let it get into you. In college, I had two professors who were both members of a false belief system. After a lecture in which both spent a lot of time pointing out the fallacies of their religion, I asked, "If the roots of your religion are so filled with fallacy, why are you a part of it?" Both answered, "Because it is a good place to raise my family." I realized that they, as well as many others, were not a part of their faith communities because they believed it to be truth but because they believed it to be practical. Both professors sacrificed reason and truth to engage what they felt was beneficial to their family. This drove me to look at why I did what I did. Why was I a believer in Jesus? Here is my conclusion that I know will make some angry. My religion is better because it is truth that works. I have not had to sacrifice reason for practice. The Word of God is truth that works, so if you get into it in such a way that it gets into you, it will change and transform you and produce the best possible life.

## THE BIBLE IS ALIVE AND ACTIVE

*Hebrews 4:12 (NIV) For the word of God is alive and active. Sharper than any double-edged sword, it penetrates even to dividing soul and spirit, joints and marrow; it judges the thoughts and attitudes of the heart.*

As a child, I was trained to always end my prayer with the phrase, "In Jesus' name." I remember thinking how sad it was that God would not hear the prayer of believers who prayed without this formula. It was as a young person doing a study over prayer that I realized that the phrase "in the name of" was not some charm but a reference to authority and power. When a Roman general stood before a city demanding surrender in the name of Caesar, his words carried the weight of an entire army that was poised and ready to force compliance. Similarly, the name of Jesus was a reference to the power of God being displayed on earth. When Christians pray in obedience to the commands of Christ, they have the authority of the risen Lord who said, "All authority is given me in heaven and upon earth" (Matthew 28:18). His authority is as alive and active today as it was 2000 years ago, for scripture says that one day "at the name of Jesus every knee will bow and every tongue confess that He is Lord" (Philippians 2:10). By alive and active, the writer of Hebrews is not saying that the words themselves are alive as if they are spell-casting tools. No, the Bible is not a book of enchantments that have life in themselves, but it is alive and active because the One who speaks it is alive and active. In Jesus' name means that the Almighty God of the universe is alive, real, active, and ready to bring the weight of His power and might to bear on my and your problems.

You cannot divorce the idea of a living, active word from the one who speaks it. Just like sticks and stones can break bones, words from the right person can hurt. I have seen destinies of sons determined by the words of their fathers. I have seen the futures of daughters limited by the words of their mothers. I have counseled grown men who weep like babies when they quote the negative words spoken to them by their mother or father as a child. Often it seems that time does not heal all hurts—it only amplifies them. On the other hand, I have seen both men and women secure, certain, and confident in their God-given abilities because of the affirming words of mom and dad as they were growing up. If the words of parents remain alive and active, affecting the lives of children for years, how much more are the Words of God capable of affecting our lives from now to eternity? Words are powerful from the right people. God's Word is active and alive because He is active and alive. God's words are, as He is, truth that cannot be avoided but must be dealt with. Like Adam and Eve, you can cover your nakedness with leaves and hide in the garden, but the living and active God still speaks your name and reveals the truth about you.

> *Like a virus that infects, permeates, and reproduces, truth always strives to change its host.*

God's Word is alive and active because it is truth. Like a virus that infects, permeates, and reproduces, truth always strives to change its host. On the other hand, just like exposure to a little of a virus can make you immune to the virus itself, many people who are regularly exposed to the truth of God's Word build an increasing immunity to its effects. By continually disregarding the application of truth, they have taught themselves how to hear and even acknowledge it as truth without allowing permeation and transformation. Week after week, they have learned how to hear without really hearing. They can talk about sin in general without ever looking at their own sin and debate the problems of the world without considering their own spiritually disabling issues. They can strain at a gnat while swallowing a camel and can point out a splinter without seeing their own plank.

On the other hand, like a virus that invades, permeates, and changes its host, the truth of God, if allowed in, will change the Christian from the inside out. If you get into it, it will get into you. If you read it with an open heart, it will open you up and read you. God's truth, allowed to run its course, will show you the wrong things you are doing and teach you the right things to do. This truth in you, in conjunction with the Spirit of God, can permeate, reproduce, and empower you to avoid wrong and do right. Long-term exposure to the alive and active truth of God will produce Christ-like character.

## THE BIBLE IS SHARP: LIKE A SHARP KNIFE

The Word of God is sharper than a scalpel. When I was a boy, my dad would occasionally bring his knife and whetstone to the kitchen table and sharpen the knife to the point you could shave with it. It was almost surgically sharp. As believers, we need the sharp truth of God to expose the sin that keeps us from reaching the full potential that God created and saved us for. Like kids playing with fire, we have played with sin to the point it has burned us. Like a surgeon, God in His mercy uses His Word to expose and cut away the deadness and in His grace grafts new flesh that makes us like Christ.

Just like a sharp blade, God's Word penetrates, slices, separates, and exposes. But then again, this is what truth does. Just like the scalpel in a surgeon's hand, God's Word is truth that penetrates below all self-deception, slices and separates it from healthy tissues, and exposes it for the cancer it is. Like most surgeries, this is painful but needful for healthy Christ-like living.

In order for God's Word to change you, you must believe that every time you open and read it, God is speaking to you. You must stop dabbling in it as a witticism for your daily or weekly life. You must stop reading it for just knowledge's sake and start reading it to know HIM. You must stop reading it as your first task of the day and start reading it as an encounter with the Living GOD. You must suckle it as a newborn baby *(1 Peter 2:2)*, feast upon it as starving man, and drink it like parched traveler because it comes from the Bread of Life and the Living Water.

Getting the Word into people is the work of the Holy Spirit facilitated by a Spirit-filled believer. We expose people to the Word so that the Holy Spirit will expose them to God and His objective and subjective truth and bring them to a point of decision. This decision always involves greater intimacy with God, movement toward deeper transformation, and greater understanding of His will for our lives. Jesus said that if you follow His teaching, you will know the truth and the truth will set you free. Hebrews tells us the Word of God is sharper than a sword that cuts both ways and is able to filet and lay open before God all motives and intents.

This mantra is the focus of the next three sections of this book. In the first, we will talk about getting people into the Word. In the second, we will discuss getting the Word into people. In the third, we will deal with monitoring and maintaining this process in the life of an individual so that they become more and more like Christ.

# SECTION 2: GETTING PEOPLE INTO THE WORD

## CHAPTER 7: START WITH JESUS

Where do we start this process of getting someone into the Word? As a church planter, pastor, and missionary, I have knocked on a lot of doors. I have cold called more than Frosty the Snowman. I have met people in their pajamas, in their work clothes, in their play clothes, and, a couple of times, in very few clothes at all. I have been physically attacked by dogs and verbally by people. In addition to cold calls, I have used mail outs, banners, T-shirts, gift bags, and door hangers to get the attention of my community. What I have found is that different people respond to different things. As a 32-year-old pastor of a transitional church that had a median age of 63 in a community with a median age of 34, I really began to understand how different people responded to different ways of contact. While my older people loved me to cold call, my younger people were almost offended by it. For my older people, who were raised in the days before house phones, when contact was always personal, dropping by unannounced was commonplace, often encouraged, or expected. On the other hand, my younger people who grew up with house phones, then later cell phones, emails, and text messaging, would think it rude to drop by without contacting them first. Neither group was right or wrong; they were just different in their backgrounds, culture, and, thus, expectations. While some people love unannounced and unexpected visits, others do not. While some love to meet in the home and eat meals, other would prefer to meet in restaurants. In the same way, I have noticed that finding the person to begin this process with can be very different in different environments and cultures. The point is that different people require different methods of contact to enter a process of discipleship.

> *If Jesus died for all, why can't we just start with one.*

One characteristic is common to all methods. We must GO! Every receptive person is out there in the world before they are in here in the church. Most every person I have encountered within my church was first cultivated by someone outside the church. My signs, banners, or mail outs may have helped, but someone did the groundbreaking work in their life. Someone went to them. Until all Christians are trained to be disciples to the point of becoming disciple makers, until Christians begin to see their home place, work place, and play place as the mission fields that God has sent them to, we will never see a movement of God that penetrates the growing demand of lostness. The same Jesus who sent the twelve in Luke 9 and the 70 in Luke 10 is sending you. Start means GO!

"Go" is the example set for us by Jesus. Philippians 2:5-11 is all about Jesus leaving heaven (Go) to come to earth, and although this sacrifice would have be great in itself, Paul adds that Jesus' going included the cross. If the God of the universe, Ruler of all things, Almighty, Lord of Lords, and King of Kings could GO from heaven to the cross, why can't we go to a neighbor or the person in the cubicle next to us? If Jesus died for all, why can't we just start with one?

The book of Luke is the prequel to Acts. The teachings and practices of Jesus are the foundation for the book of Acts. Maybe one reason the church is losing ground today is that we know how to grow a church but we have forgotten how to start it. The starting place for the church was the Gospels, not Acts; Jesus laid the foundation. This is important to understand because more and more we are living in less and less of a Christian world. Nowadays, we are living in a world that is more similar to the pagan world of the first century. Thus, we must learn how to bake Christians from scratch. The ready mix church-in-a-box Christianity, *If I build it they will come*, that we have used to get people to church will not work in a world so far removed from the Gospel. While my father's generation was likely to wake up on Sunday and say, "Let's go to church," while my generation would say, "Let's go BACK to church," and while my children's generation would say, "Let's TRY church," today's Millennials are very likely to say, "What's church?" Although spirituality is important to many of the people who live in our world today, it is not reserved for Christianity.

> Although spirituality is important to many of the people who live in our world today, it is not reserved for Christianity.

The next big wave of growth in your church, the solution to your declining membership, and the changes needed to bring renewal may not be found within the walls of your church. It may be found outside the walls with a new wave of the redeemed; it may start with the Gospels and Jesus' teaching on going and finding the person of peace. Without discounting the work of the Holy Spirit in Acts, maybe we need to look at the work of Jesus first.

If you asked Jesus about going, about starting this process, I believe His answer would be similar to the commissioning and sending of His apostles and disciples in the Gospels. This was Jesus' *cook from scratch* method. The rabbinic approach to teaching, which Jesus used to train His disciples, included teaching, modeling, doing, and then debriefing, which included even further teaching. In the Gospels we see Jesus doing this with the 12 apostles and then again with 70 disciples. Using Matthew 10 as our main passage, supported by Luke and Mark, we will look at what Jesus teaches us about going and how it can help us in the creation of a transformative culture.

# CHAPTER 8: START WHERE PEOPLE ARE: HANG OUT WITH LOST PEOPLE

*Luke 10: 1 (NIV) After this the Lord appointed seventy-two others and sent them two by two ahead of him to every town and place where he was about to go. 2 He told them, "The harvest is plentiful, but the workers are few. Ask the Lord of the harvest, therefore, to send out workers into his harvest field.*

Jesus sent His disciples two by two into the populated areas of this world. He sent them to where the people were. He sent them in advance to prepare people for His coming. My group of Christians has traditionally been good at planting churches in rural environments; also, planting Boomer churches in the suburbs has met with some success. We have, however, lacked in our ability to  penetrate cities and large metropolitan areas—where 81% of people of the US live. Most of my ministry has been in these great areas of need and, for the last 20+ years, outside of the Bible Belt, in Southern California and Northeastern Ohio. My previous ministry area included 1.3 million people with 24 churches in my service area. Of these churches 3 averaged 150-200 in attendance, most averaged below 100, and the rest averaged below 50. When you consider that my group is the largest Protestant denomination in the US and we have only one church for every 52,000 people in my area, you get a sense of this great need.

In addition, in all the surveys I have done for churches I have served, only ¼ of the community considered themselves to be of a strong faith involvement while the rest considered themselves to be of moderate to none, with only 1 or 2 out of ten going to church on any given Sunday. To help my churches become more aware of the lostness around them, I have asked congregants to envision their neighborhood and, picturing the 4 to 5 homes on each side of theirs, to raise their hand if they know ONE neighbor who went to church that morning. Most do not, and if I ask if they are aware of TWO, all but a very few will lower their hands. These urban areas are filled with some of the most under-reached people of our day, and although the demographics and lifestyle are different, they have one thing in common: more and more they think less and less about church and God as we do. We are only one generation away from a pagan society: that generation lives in these areas. Reaching them requires Christians being willing to go, live, work, and play among them, scattering a lot of seed while looking for receptive hearts.

The imagery that is used often by Jesus in the New Testament is one of sowing, but sowing is not the same as planting. While planting places an individual seed in the ground, evenly spaced and in rows, sowing is the broadcasting of seed that requires a lot of seed and land. We plant corn and peas, while we sow wheat and grass. This image of sowing is more in line with the way we start the process of creating a transformative culture. In order for this to happen, we need to cast a lot of seed. We need to put ourselves in places where we can engage many people in multiple conversations until we find that one whom God has prepared. I recently read that 85% of the people, if you can stop them long enough to engage them in conversation, will have spiritual conversations with you.

> *Jesus was truly a man of the people without being the politician*

Notice I am not talking about a mail out to thousands of people or a banner that hundreds may drive by and see or even a billboard that thousands can observe on their way to work. I am not talking about the hundreds that just read your blog or Facebook postings. What I am talking about is many personal conversations, one-on-one. The goal is face-to-face contact. Although the encounters may start up using technology such as Facebook, emails, and texting, it is still about personal contact.

Jesus was all about people. In Philippians the 2nd chapter, we see Jesus as an expert on God and an expert on humanity. As much as Jesus knew about God because He was God, He also knew about humanity because He created us and became human. But not only did He know humanity because He was human, He also knew humanity because He hung out with humans. Jesus was truly a man of the people without being the politician.

For most of us, especially those who are more introverted, people energy is a limited resource. This is why many pastors and church workers take naps on Sunday afternoon. The busy schedule of many churches can be counter-productive to the outreach of a church because our limited people energy is used up hanging out with Christians. To start a transformative culture, we must stop babysitting Christians and invest more time and energy in lost people. This means we must free up our limited time and energy to prioritize lostness the way God does.

The main idea of the three parables of Luke 15 is the importance of lostness. Heaven celebrates when the lost are found more than it celebrates the continuing security of those who are already there. One lost coin out of 10, one lost sheep out of 100, and one lost son out of 2 are illustrations of the fact that God considered lostness as significant. If God places such a high value on lost people, shouldn't we? If Jesus gave up heaven and came to earth to spend His days hanging out with lost people, shouldn't we carve out significant time from our busy schedules to make lost people a priority? If we are to be like Jesus, we must be willing to not only give UP OUR LIFE for people, we must also be willing to give OF OUR LIFE to hang out with people.

## CHAPTER 9: LIMIT YOUR FOCUS: START WITH **YOUR** PEOPLE GROUP

*Matthew 10: 5-6 (NIV) These twelve Jesus sent out with the following instructions: "Do not go among the Gentiles or enter any town of the Samaritans. 6 Go rather to the lost sheep of Israel.*

*Start at home, in a homeland among your people,* were the instructions of Jesus as He sent His followers out. Given their time, talents, and experience, limiting their scope to their homeland focused their efforts and gave them experiences that could be used by Jesus in their ongoing development.

Jesus modeled for us how to live for God with human limitations. Although Jesus was God in the flesh and bone, being the incarnate Christ meant taking on certain limitations of the human form. Jesus always handled these limitations with precision, accuracy, and perfection. He took His limited time on earth and never missed an appointment. He took all the limitations of a frail human body but never missed an opportunity to teach or serve those He encountered. Even His death, burial, and resurrection were perfectly timed to be the climax of His teaching and ministry on Earth. Jesus always knew what His physical limitations were, and He always knew what His disciples could handle, too. Jesus never traveled more than 120 miles from His place of birth, yet what He did with His physical limitations in this limited environment turned the world upside down and changed it forever.

God may impose limitations on us for several reasons. God uses limits to test our ability to handle future responsibility, to see how we would do with the little before He gives us more. Again, God knows what we are capable of; therefore, He tests us not for His information but for our understanding of ourselves. Like lower ranking officers in the military engage their missions without knowing the greater strategies of commanding officers, God may be giving us just enough to do what needs to be done in our area of Kingdom work. He may do this to test our abilities before giving us more responsibility and greater understanding of His purpose. Similar to testing, limiting our focus at times will help us create a reproducible pattern. God sometimes calls us to develop our skills on a small scale before giving us the opportunity to use our abilities on a larger scale. This was taught by Jesus through the Parable of the Talents and again when He talks about the Shrewd Manager. Observe what Jesus says in Luke.

*Luke 16:10 "If you are faithful in little things, you will be faithful in large ones. But if you are dishonest in little things, you won't be honest with greater responsibilities. 11 And if you are untrustworthy about worldly wealth, who will trust you with the true riches of heaven? 12 And if you are not faithful with other people's things, why should you be trusted with things of your own?"*

Focus may be another reason for limits. At times, limits may be imposed by God to help us focus on what God knows we can achieve and to prevent us from being distracted or overwhelmed by the big picture. How do you eat an elephant? One bite at a time. Most mature Christians will tell you that it is a good thing that God did not give them the big picture all at once but instead bits and pieces as they needed them. God has continually limited me to the places where I could be most effective, given my time, talents, gifts, and treasures at that time. These limitations that produce greater focus can help us penetrate more and go deeper before we go broader. Like a good foundation, we have to build down before we can build up and out. Needless to say, limits are not bad things, and God often uses them as training tools. Jesus limited His disciples to the lost sheep of Israel not because He did not care about the rest of the world but to prepare them for the rest of the world.

To test us, to bring greater awareness of self, or to maintain focus for creating a pattern for effective growth are why God limits our scope and why Jesus limited the disciples to the lost sheep of Israel. Israel was the testing ground where disciples were appraised, refined, and prepared for kingdom expansion. In a way, their going to the lost sheep of Israel is the parallel to Jerusalem as mentioned in Acts 1:8. Just as the disciples were limited to Judea, the church was limited to Jerusalem as the testing ground for new recruits. It was in the limited geography of Jerusalem that the new believers could focus on Jesus' teaching and on developing their skills before they were launched by persecution into Judea, Samaria, and the ends of the earth.

Another reason that Jesus limited His disciples to working with the lost sheep of Israel is that these were their people. With the exception of those who possess the missionary gift, most of us will work best with people like ourselves. People who speak the same language, have similar backgrounds, and face the same struggles are the easiest people for me to connect with and engage with the Gospel. It is interesting how God used this principle after the event of Pentecost to get His message to the world. At Pentecost, there were thousands of Hellenistic Jews who came to know the Lord under the leadership of the Judean disciples. Although they were religiously Jews, they were culturally different from the Jewish people of Judea. These Hellenistic Jews were often multi-lingual in that they knew Greek and the language of their native regions, perhaps could read Hebrew from their training in the Synagogues, and maybe even spoke Aramaic, the predominant language of Judea. In short, they were the perfect missionaries to take the Gospel home to their native lands. God brought them together at Pentecost, saved them, equipped them through the Judean disciples' and the Apostles' ministry, and then through persecution launched them out, many going back to their homes where they took the Good News of Jesus with them. Like Paul, these multilingual, multicultural Hellenistic Jews were better suited than their Judean brothers and sisters to take the Gospel to a Greek-speaking world and were specifically suited to take this life-changing message back their own homes. Jerusalem became the testing ground, training ground, and launching pad for the church.

Christians today are more united than ever in our goal to reach the world for Christ, as we should be. It is right that we join together to support missionaries and mission efforts around the world. However, for the *individual* Christian, the idea of reaching the uttermost parts of the world may be overwhelming. Maybe the answer to this monumental task of reaching the world is to start with our little corner of it. If everyone in my house would clean up their own rooms, 80% of my house would be clean (then on to the garage). I have always noticed that one of the great transformative powers of a mission trip is its ability to teach individuals that what they can do in a foreign land they can and should do at home. These individuals had to go to the ends of the earth in order to see and engage the lostness in their backyard.

God never intended for you to reach the world for Christ (now you're off the hook); He does, however, intend for you to reach the people in your sphere of influence (oops, now you're back on). What if every Christian focused their attention on one receptive person in their home place, play place, or work place? What would your church look like in a year? What if one Christian engaged one person for one year in a discipleship relationship, teaching them to the point of reproduction? After the first year, you would have two discplers doing the same thing. After two years you would have 4 and in 10 years 256. What is amazing is that if one person, starting with one person, would accomplish this Great Commission (Matthew 28:18-20) of making disciples through going, baptizing, and then teaching them to obey all that Jesus commanded, then in 20 years that one person would have created a movement of over 500,000 individuals. Stop being overwhelmed by the world, limit your focus, and start with your people.

## CHAPTER 10: GO LIKE JESUS

*Matthew 10:8 (NIV) Heal the sick, raise the dead, cleanse those who have leprosy, drive out demons. Freely you have received, freely give.*

### MEET THE NEEDS OF OTHERS

Healing the sick, raising the dead, cleansing those with leprosy, driving out demons—these were all abilities of Jesus, which He gave to His disciples. When Jesus sent His disciples out, He sent them out to do the things He did. Jesus freely met people's needs, and He expected His disciples to do the same. Freely meeting needs is an important part of being a Christian.

"Freely" means without conditions or strings attached. Jesus reminded His disciples that what He lavished on them should be given to others with the same generous spirit.

These gifts are also accompanied by the command to take nothing, eat what was set before you, and stay where people will have you. In other words, just like Jesus Himself, He sent His disciples with little or no overhead. Could it be that in the church today this time of free giving is difficult? With buildings and budgets comes the need for bigger offerings and more investors; these needs can permeate every aspect of ministry, if not in reality, then in perception. I have personally sat in on financial meetings where outreach was discussed as an avenue for fundraising. While buildings and budgets can be assets, they must never be the motivation for reaching more people. The physical and financial burdens that we create for ourselves can distort the real motive of love. The real question is when the church serves others, do the people we serve feel it is unconditional or do they feel they have just paid for a pitch? While meeting the needs of people is a ministry of the church, we should always do it in a way that is free of strings.

## DEPEND ON GOD

*Matthew 10:9-10 (NIV) Do not take along any gold or silver or copper in your belts; 10 take no bag for the journey, or extra tunic, or sandals or a staff;*

Jesus stands as an example of someone who completely depended on God.

Going means depending on God. Although I have known fishermen that have been so confident in their ability to catch fish they wouldn't take any food with them, I've never been so confident in my fishing ability. Trusting in my ability to eat what I catch would have turned most of my fishing trips into fasts. Not taking any money, luggage, extra clothes, or a walking stick in their service to God meant that the disciples would have to depend upon Him for their needs. I am not using this as an argument for full-time ministry but simply as an argument for dependence on and faith in the One who sends us—the One to whom we are to pray: give *us this* **day** *our* **daily** *bread*.

In order to depend upon God, we must stop depending on things. Notice Jesus had the power of God, displayed in some impressive abilities to meet the needs of people, but He had no place to live. As a matter of fact, after three years of ministry, Jesus had nothing of this world except His relationship with God, which He came to earth with, and the followers He developed here on earth. While most would see the lack of things as a sign of failure, others might see it as a sign of focus. Howard Hendricks says that the secret of concentration is elimination. Great things for God require great sacrifice. Following Jesus required leaving nets, boats, money, and causes behind. It is not a matter of doing more with less; it is doing more because we have less. The less I have, the less I have to maintain; the less I maintain, the more time I have to invest in things that really matter. To have more of the things that really matter, I need less of things that don't.

Going like Jesus means decluttering our lives. In my attempt to organize my life to be more productive, I have come to believe that at least one definition of clutter is resources that cannot be accessed in a reasonable time frame. Let's face it. The pile of papers we have saved on our desk that we call resources, items we may need someday, is just clutter. The things that I am saving to be more productive are actually preventing productivity. This is also true for my life; many of the things that I say I need prevent me from seeing the things that I really need. I am convicted by the idea that the clutter of my life may make it difficult for me to do what God would have me do. I am not just talking about the luxuries of my life but also the things I would consider needs that at times stop me from depending on God. Money, luggage, and extra clothes are all things I consider as needs, but Jesus considered them clutter. If it is true that we came into this world with nothing and we will leave this world with nothing, then is it also not true that many of the things we gather while we are here in this world are temporary and could be defined as clutter?

Having too much stuff is distracting and will stop us from meeting the needs of others. It is in our dependence on God that we find the resources to help others. The branch that is dependent on the resources provided by the vine is the one that produces, according to Jesus in John 15. In this context, abiding is dependence and the only way to be fruitful as a Christian.

## FOCUSED ON GOD'S WORK

*Matthew 10: 9-10 (NIV) Do not take along any gold or silver or copper in your belts; 10 take no bag for the journey, or extra tunic, or sandals or a staff;* **for the worker is worth his keep.**

When our lives become uncluttered with the unimportant, we can see the things that really matter and do the work that really makes a difference. I am sure that even as a carpenter helping His father with building projects, Jesus knew what His real job on earth was. As a twelve-year-old child, His response to His parents' rebuke, after they frantically searched for Him and found Him in the Temple, was, "Wouldn't you have expected me to be about my Father's affairs?" Isn't the same true for us? Maybe the real question is: who are you really working for? Who is the real boss? Isn't it God who gives life, energy, natural abilities, and learned skills, which are actually what your employer is paying you for? Without God's life sustaining power, we have nothing to offer an employer. So doing the work of your employer without regard for God and His work does not make sense.

So, what does make sense? God's redemptive work, helping others to discover the intimate relationship that God desires with them, is the ultimate purpose of life. Knowing God the Creator is the avenue for knowing the purpose of all creation. Knowing God helps me answer the great questions of life such as *Why am I here? What is the purpose of my life?* Although the specifics of this question are between you and God, the general answer is the same for all Christians. Just like He sent Jesus, God has sent you to do His work—the work or ministry of reconciliation (2 Corinthians 5:11-21). Having found the Living Water of Jesus Christ, it is the responsibility of every Christian to share it with every individual in a drought-stricken world. As a Christian, this work is more important than making money and providing for your physical needs. It is more important because it has eternal consequences. It is important because it is beneficial here on earth. It is the difference between living and good living, between living a life of survival and a life of significance. I do not believe that Matthew the Tax Collector regretted leaving his money table behind or that Peter, James, and John regretted leaving their nets behind for the adventure Jesus had for them. Even with all the pain and suffering they bore, I believe they would say, emphatically, the words written by Rhea F. Miller and popularized by George Beverly Shea during the Billy Graham Evangelistic Crusades:

> I'd rather have Jesus than silver or gold;
> I'd rather be His than have riches untold;
> I'd rather have Jesus than houses or lands,
> I'd rather be led by His nail pierced hand.
>
> Than to be a king of a vast domain
> Or be held in sin's dread sway,
> I'd rather have Jesus than anything
> This world affords today.
>
> I'd rather have Jesus than men's applause;
> I'd rather be faithful to His dear cause;
> I'd rather have Jesus than world-wide fame,
> I'd rather be true to His holy name.
>
> He's fairer than lilies of rarest bloom;
> He's sweeter than honey from out of the comb;
> He's all that my hungering spirit needs,
> I'd rather have Jesus and let Him lead.

You are not a worker who is also a Christian; you are a Christian worker, whose work place is his mission field. God did not give you time, talents, and treasure so you can work, retire, and die. God's redeeming work is the worker who *is worth his keep*.

Being like Jesus means making God's work a priority. An uncluttered life that is dependent upon God frees us to do whatever God would have us do. Remember that Jesus is talking to fishermen, a tax collector, and a zealot about a whole new profession. Maybe Christians would do well if they understood that becoming a follower of Christ is taking on a new profession, a career choice instead of a task. It seems that for the average Christian there is much more effort put into their work place than their Christian life. If you ask them why, they would probably say that their job provides them with the things they need. Wow, I thought God did that. Please note that I am not talking about you leaving your job for full-time ministry but about making God's work a priority in the job that you have been given by God to do, making your work place your mission field.

> **Man shall not live by bread alone or by focusing all his attention on the job that gives him that bread.**

Jesus saw the work of God as being as satisfying for the soul as food is for the body. In John 4:34 (NIV), Jesus said that His *"food . . . is to do the will of him who sent me and to finish his work."* The real provision that sustains life is not found in your job but in your relationship with God and others. Man shall not live by bread alone or by focusing all his attention on the job that gives him that bread. Jesus tells us in Matthew 6 to stop worrying about the needs of life (and, by inference, the job that we do to provide for those needs) and, instead, focus on God's kingdom, and He will meet our needs.

*Matthew 6:33 (NIV 84) But seek first his kingdom and his righteousness, and all these things will be given to you as well.*

## CHAPTER 11: WANTED: RECEPTIVE PEOPLE

*Luke 10:5–8 (NIV 84) 5 "When you enter a house, first say, 'Peace to this house.' 6 If a man of peace is there, your peace will rest on him; if not, it will return to you."*

*Matthew 10:11-13 (NIV) "Whatever town or village you enter, search for some worthy person there and stay at his house until you leave. 12 As you enter the home, give it your greeting. 13 If the home is deserving let your peace rest on it; if it is not, let your peace return to you."*

Jesus did not commission His followers to find a crowd and preach to them. No, He told them to find the ONE—the one who could open the door to many. The first person you will need to get into the Word is the person of peace. The literal translation for this is *son of peace*. In both the New and Old Testament, the word "son" was used to describe many things, from national affiliation such as the "sons of Israel," to tribal affiliation such as the "sons of Judah," or to family affiliation such as the "sons of Jesse." It was also used to describe the character of a person both negative and positive. Jesus, on one occasion, refers to false teachers as "sons of the devil" and another time "sons of perdition." Christians are referred to as "sons of light" and challenged to be "sons of encouragement." Jesus in the passage above tells His disciples to seek out the one who is characterized by peace or the son of peace.

The need for peace is a product of being at war. The peace that Jesus is referring to is not that of a world free of war, nor is He talking about the peace that is needed in the conflicts among men. Instead, He is referring to the peace that is needed between man, the sinner, and God, the righteous. The son of peace is the one who understands this conflict and is seeking inner peace. This is the person whom the Spirit has been working on prior to your arrival, convicting and convincing him or her of sin, righteousness, and judgment.

*John 16:8-11 (NIV) When he comes, he will prove the world to be in the wrong about sin and righteousness and judgment: 9 about sin, because people do not believe in me; 10 about righteousness, because I am going to the Father, where you can see me no longer; 11 and about judgment, because the prince of this world now stands condemned.*

Because of the work of the Holy Spirit, the person of peace knows something is wrong, and this understanding produces conflict in his soul. It is the Holy Spirit's convincing a person of their sin, God's righteousness, and impending judgment that creates receptivity to you and your message. It is on this desire for peace inside them that your peace can rest (Matthew 10). You have the Gospel—the Good News—the message of peace—that they need.

Most of us who have been driving for any period of time understand the conflict that is produced by sin, righteousness, and judgment. We have all passed a patrol officer on the interstate, looked down at our speedometer, and felt the guilt that comes from driving 10, 15, or 20 MPH over the speed limit. In a split second, we are convinced of sin, righteousness, and coming judgment. For the next few miles, we are in conflict as we fearfully look back in our mirror, praying that the officer was distracted by something or someone else. The conflict intensifies when we see the lights come on and he begins moving our direction, but we still hope that it is the guy in front or behind that he is after. All hope feels lost, however, to impending judgment when the righteous cop pulls behind me, the sinner. When he steps to the window of my car, sin, righteousness, judgment, and the conflict they create make my heart race and my palms sweaty with guilt and condemnation. I am wrong, he is right, and I deserve a ticket.

Although I expect this message from him, what if he gives me a warning? What if His message for me is one of forgiveness, not judgment? This is message I want, I need; this is the message that I am ready to hear. "I am just going to give you a warning this time" is the message to me that abates the conflict within and brings peace to my soul. It puts things right between me and the law. My record is clean, not because I deserve it, but because I have been forgiven. In the same way, the Holy Spirit works in the hearts of men preparing them for the message of peace, the Gospel. He convinces them of their imperfection, and this imperfection, as small as they might perceive it to be, separates them from a perfect God. This truth makes them receptive to the message of forgiveness that gives them a clean record, not because they deserve it but because they have been forgiven.

Matthew describes this same idea by referring to a receptive individual as a *worthy* person. By worthy, he's not referring to the deserving person, like the Boy Scout who has earned his merit badge. Like the person of peace, Jesus is referring to a receptive person who matches or balances your message that the "Kingdom of God is near." The word "worthy" actually has its roots in the idea of weights and measures. An item would be placed on one side of a set of scales, and then weights would be placed on the other side to counterbalance the items until the scales balanced. The amount of weight needed to balance was the measure of the item. These weights were comparable or fitting for the item being weighed.

> *I am saddened by the idea that Holy Spirit is preparing hearts for the message I am not sharing, all because I lack surrender to the same Spirit.*

Today this picture is relevant to say the least. On the scales of life, the lost person is weighted down by sin. This condition, revealed by the Holy Spirit, can be brought into balance only by King Jesus and His forgiveness. This is the nearness of the Kingdom that is only a prayer of surrender away. When Jesus tells His disciples to look for the worthy one, He's telling them to look for the one whom the Spirit has prepared for this message: King Jesus is near. So then, when Jesus refers to a worthy person, He's not talking about a deserving person but one who is open and receptive to the message.

The ramifications of this are powerfully convicting. If we believe that the Holy Spirit is at work, daily convincing people of their need for forgiveness, preparing them and making them receptive, then it would stand to reason that God is regularly putting such a person of peace in my path or in our paths as Christians. I am saddened by the idea that the Holy Spirit is preparing hearts for the message I am not sharing, all because I lack surrender to the same Spirit.

A person of peace is the first receptive person of influence in a community, the first supporter of your ministry, and the gatekeeper to his or her people group. He or she is the spark to igniting a movement of God in a community; he or she is the first that leads to the second and third and so on and so on.

# CHAPTER 12: CHARACTERISTICS OF THE PERSON OF PEACE

When we talk about characteristics in regard to a person, we are speaking of the character of the person. Character includes the habits that are so embedded in a person that they characterize him. These traits are so embedded in a person's thinking and behavior that they may be surprised to hear someone else articulate them. Thus, the person of peace does not see themselves as a person of peace, and if you ask for a volunteer from the audience, they would not step forward. Because of this, you need to know what you are looking for as you seek the person of peace, and you may, on some level, have to help them realize how God desires to use the qualities that you see in them. The list below is a guide to help in your pursuit of the ONE, the person of peace that starts the movement.

## THEY ARE SEEKERS OF THE TRUTH

Maybe it was all the so-called truth they have acted on that just did not work, but the person of peace is often a person frustrated by other spiritual pursuits. They cannot accept the world's unrestrained liberalism, and they cannot live up to the strenuous demands of legalism. Whatever the case, they are dissatisfied with all other attempts to know God or their gods. They are not satisfied with attributing creation to the creature. They know that where there is design there is designer, where there is a building there is a builder, and where there is order there is an organizer; and they have a God given desire to know the designer, builder, and organizer of all things.

## THEY ARE HIGHLY RECEPTIVE AND RESPONSIVE

Persons of peace are receptive to spiritual matters. They desire to know more; they are continual learners. They are the prepared soil that is willing for God to deal with hardness, with hidden rocks below the surface, and with distractions that keep them from developing roots and bearing fruit.

Not all receptive persons of peace are lost. Some are saved but have never been challenged to develop, mature, and grow as Christians. Others have experienced discipleship but have never been challenged to Go. Others may have done much of the work in a person's life prior to our arrival. We may, as Jesus said, be harvesting where we have not planted or planting where we will not harvest. An example of this is 1 Cor. 3 where Paul says, "I planted,

Apollos watered, but God gives the increase." Therefore, as we approach a person, we must be prepared to move them on in one of three areas: Gospel, Grow, or Go.

## THEY ARE OPTIMISTIC—HOPEFUL OF CHANGE

I have never seen a bitter, angry person as a person of peace. He is called the person of peace for a reason. Even before this person experiences the peace of God, even before forgiveness is experienced that brings about the peace between God and the person, he expresses a form of peace. This peace is expressed in hope. By hope, I do not mean "maybe it will or maybe it won't." I mean the biblical definition of hope, which defines hope as an expectation and anticipation of God's work. Cornelius was a hopeful person of peace who had been prepared by the Holy Spirit to receive the message of Peter. As Cornelius looked to Peter with hope and expectation, the person of peace will look to you expecting to hear from God.

## THEY ARE HOSPITABLE

*Luke 10: 4-7 (NIV) Do not take a purse or bag or sandals; and do not greet anyone on the road. 5 "When you enter a house, first say, 'Peace to this house.' 6 If someone who promotes peace is there, your peace will rest on them; if not, it will return to you. 7 Stay there, eating and drinking whatever they give you, for the worker deserves his wages. Do not move around from house to house.*

In the above passage, Jesus prohibits His disciples from taking anything extra to provide for future needs. Similarly, Jesus had told his apostles, as he sent them, "*Do not get any gold or silver or copper to take with you in your belts— 10 no bag for the journey or extra shirt or sandals or a staff, for the worker is worth his keep*" (Matthew 10:9-10 NIV). So we see Jesus is directing His followers to go and count on the hospitality of the others. He is sending them with the great need to be dependent on the ministry (their work) and on the person of peace to provide for their needs. While most guests are like fish and often stink after a few days, these men were welcomed into the homes of these individuals as one of their own. Giving, sharing, and providing for the needs of the ones sent by Jesus was, for the person of peace, a way of participating in Kingdom work.

The person of peace must be from my tribe because where we meet we eat. Throughout the Gospels, hospitality seems to characterize the person of peace. They will feed you, they will meet your needs, and they will invest in you and your ministry.

## THEY ARE PERSONS OF INFLUENCE—GATEKEEPERS

The person of peace is the first wave of change; when they surrender, it often starts the next wave. Jesus does not tell His disciples to go and find **people** of peace; He tells them to go and find the **person** of peace (Luke 10:6).

In Luke 10:2 Jesus begins His dialogue with His followers talking about the limited laborers in the midst of a languishing harvest.

*Luke 10:2 (NIV) He told them, "The harvest is plentiful, but the workers are few. Ask the Lord of the harvest, therefore, to send out workers into his harvest field.*

Jesus sees the need for an increasing work force to meet the need of a ripe and ready harvest, but where are they to come from? Where do we get these harvesters? The answer is found in the person of peace. These individuals are not just the first to be harvested; they are the first to be equipped and deployed back into the harvest. This is God's answer. He is the Lord of the Harvest who turns the harvest into harvesters. God looked and saw a "mighty warrior" in Gideon while he was hiding from the Midianites; He saw Fishers of Men in fishermen; He saw Paul the Missionary in Saul, the merciless persecutor of the church. Likewise, God sees in the harvest the harvester, in the fruit the fruitful, and in the product the producer. Just like in every fruit are the seeds of the next harvest, in every person of peace are the seeds of the next gathering of souls.

This prayer to the Lord of the Harvest is not for the harvest itself but for the resources to gather the harvest. Now we know the harvest is a reference to people who need to hear while the laborers are people who are ready to share. Therefore, it is not a hard leap of logic to understand that on some level the prayer to the Lord of the Harvest is to make the hearers into the sharers. In other words, as you and I look at the harvest, we should envision the harvester coming out of the harvest.

A prime example of this is Cornelius and his household, who were the first major harvest among the Gentiles. Cornelius was a person of peace prepared by God. He was not only the first to be harvested; he and his influence made him the first harvester among his family and friends. In this case, the time between the one being harvested and his becoming a harvester was almost immediate. His belief was the stimulus for the belief of all the others gathered in his home. Cornelius' family and friends did not become Christians through Cornelius but because of him.

> *The person of peace is the first fruit of this ripe harvest, but ripeness also indicates a readiness to reproduce.*

The person of peace is the first laborer in answer to our prayer to the Lord of the Harvest. Throughout my ministry, I have seen God bring people who I would consider gatekeepers or persons of peace. These were often new believers who, as they invited their friends and family, quickly became catalysts for a new wave of growth in our church. After seeing God do this on several occasions, we changed our strategy development. Instead of pursuing strategies that would attempt to create waves, we developed strategies that would prepare us for the waves that God created. This strategy often had as its starting point a person of peace. Bill Bright, the founder of Campus Crusade, always said, "Fruit that is ripe—you just touch it and it falls off." I would add to this that once that first fruit has fallen, you might want to get out from under the tree because more is coming. The person of peace is the first fruit of this ripe harvest, but ripeness also indicates a readiness to reproduce. Could it be through the work of the Spirit that one is being prepared to receive and engage at the same time? Can a new believer be born pregnant?

Like a virus that may be contagious only for a few days, a new Christian may only have a short period of time to influence his lost friends and family members with the good news of Jesus Christ. As they develop new relationships in the church and as old relationships pass away, the time may be short for their lost friends to be exposed to the Gospel. Remember, it was the woman at the well who infected her people with the message, *"Come, see a man who told me everything I ever did. Could this be the Messiah?"* (John 4:29).

Years ago, I learned that groups of people do not all change at the same rate and that I could preach vision and change from the pulpit until I was blue in the face, but it would never produce the group change I felt God desired for my church. So while I still used preaching to set the stage for change, I began working with individuals that were ready. What I discovered is that change happens in waves. On one end of the spectrum are the individuals or the individual who is anxious and ready to do something different, and on the other end are those who are unwilling, unready, and unreceptive. The rest fall between these two groups and will move as they see the people they consider to be influencers move. This movement happens in waves. What I learned is that if change was going to occur, I did not need to change the group; I needed the one. This first influencer was often the gatekeeper of the second wave, and within the second wave was a gatekeeper for the third, and so on. These waves of people would continually move in the direction of change until they met the resistance of the unwilling, unready, and unreceptive, but at this point those opposed to the change were in the minority with the majority moving forward. Throughout my ministry, I have led churches to make significant changes using this method of starting with the one: the first fruit of change.

## CHAPTER 13: EXAMPLES OF PERSONS OF PEACE

### MARY AND MARTHA

Luke 10 begins with Jesus appointing and sending out the 70 disciples *ahead of him to every town and place where he was about to go* (Luke 10:1) and ends with Jesus entering into the home of Mary and Martha. It is not a far leap of logic that many of the encounters after the sending of the seventy were prepared by the seventy. Mary and Martha were probably among those engaged first by one of the seventy. These women and their brother, Lazarus, were persons of peace for the disciples who were sent out and, subsequently, for Jesus and His followers. These individuals and their home became the resting place for Jesus as He traveled back and forth from Bethany to Jerusalem.

### THE WOMAN AT THE WELL

Although not part of the 70 encounters, the woman at the well is an example of a person of peace. Who would have thought that this woman with all her problems would have been such an influence for Jesus in the town of Sychar?

*John 4:28–30 (NIV) Then, leaving her water jar, the woman went back to the town and said to the people, 29 "Come, see a man who told me everything I ever did. Could this be the Christ?" 30 They came out of the town and made their way toward him.*

### CORNELIUS

One of the greatest examples of a person of peace is Cornelius. Let's look at him more carefully in relationship to being a person of peace. In this example, we get a behind the scenes look at the preparatory work of the Holy Spirit in the life of the donor (Peter) and the recipient (Cornelius). In a dream, God prepares Cornelius' heart to receive the Gospel and tells him to send for Peter. During that same time, the Holy Spirit prepares Peter's heart to deal with his prejudice, go with the servants of Cornelius, and seize the opportunity to open the door of the Gospel to the Gentiles. When Peter arrives at Cornelius' house, he finds a large number of people there waiting to receive the message of Christ. Like a dry sponge thrown into water, these people are so ready and receptive that the Holy Spirit comes upon them before Peter even finishes speaking.

One thing that is interesting is that when Cornelius' servants meet Peter, he is not in his own house. He is in the house of Simon the Tanner, and he is napping on the roof waiting for the meal. Simon must have also been a person of peace and hospitality.

## LYDIA

*Act 16:13-15 (NIV) On the Sabbath we went outside the city gate to the river, where we expected to find a place of prayer. We sat down and began to speak to the women who had gathered there. 14One of those listening was a woman from the city of Thyatira named Lydia, a dealer in purple cloth. She was a worshiper of God. The Lord opened her heart to respond to Paul's message. 15When she and the members of her household were baptized, she invited us to her home. "If you consider me a believer in the Lord," she said, "come and stay at my house." And she persuaded us.*

Lydia is an example of a person of peace. She was an affluent person in the garment trade who became a believer under the teaching of Paul. This woman of means took Paul and his companions into her house in Philippi and provided for their needs until their departure.

Throughout the Bible, we see stories of how God prepared individuals in advance of His servants' contact. Is God, who prepared the hearts of Martha and Mary, Zacchaeus, the Woman at the Well, Cornelius, and Lydia, any less active in His preparation today? Absolutely not! God who prepared the person of peace throughout scripture is no less preparing individuals today. Another way to look at this: will I be held accountable one day for people God has prepared that I never engaged, all because of the fear of rejection? How will you and I feel one day when we see, as God sees, all the persons of peace He prepared for us to encounter and then we see the plentiful harvest of souls that these persons of peace would have impacted?

# CHAPTER 14: ENGAGE THE PERSON OF PEACE: PROCLAIM THE NEARNESS OF THE KINGDOM.

*Luke 10:9 (NIV) Heal the sick who are there and tell them, 'The kingdom of God is near you.'*

*Matthew 10: 7 (NIV) As you go, preach this message: 'The kingdom of heaven is near.'*

*Matthew 10:14 (NIV) If anyone will not welcome you or listen to your words, shake the dust off your feet when you leave that home or town. 15 I tell you the truth, it will be more bearable for Sodom and Gomorrah on the day of judgment than for that town.*

Luke says Jesus sent His disciples to go to the places He was later to go to, so, in essence, Jesus sent His disciples to prepare the way for Him. Just like Air Force One is whatever aircraft the president is on, the kingdom is wherever the king is. The nearness of Jesus Christ, the King, was the message of the disciples. Is this not our message today? Are Christians not called to proclaim to a lost world that the King and His Kingdom are near? The difference today is that the King's presence is not limited by geography, distance to be traveled, or the pace of the disciples. Part of the good news we have to share is that because of Jesus, God is nearer today than when Jesus walked the earth. The presence of the King in the heart of an individual is only a prayer away. This is the driving message of Christianity. It is a message that is fit for the worthy person, for the son of peace.

As a chaplain in the Federal Bureau of Prisons, I was occasionally summoned to the segregation unit of the institution because an inmate refused to comply with an officer's request to place his hands through the window and cuff up. My message was often twofold: either surrender and cuff up or face the Special Operations Response Team (SORT) of the institution who will force compliance. My nearness was the inmate's opportunity to surrender or face judgment.

The idea of nearness is used in Luke as an opportunity, just like a superior army, when it comes near another country, gives that country an opportunity to surrender or fight back. The nearness of the kingdom of God means one of two things: surrender or judgment. It is the ministry of all Christians to share both of these alternatives. On the one hand, rejection of Jesus our King, who is near, means being held accountable and responsible for wrongdoing and misdeeds while, on the other hand, surrender seizes an opportunity to be saved and delivered from sin and its judgment, both on this earth and for eternity.

## THE KINGDOM IS NEAR: MESSAGE OF SALVATION

Jesus' desire was that His disciples would find receptive individuals who would trust Jesus and become His followers. In the first century, disciples traveled with their teachers and listened with a desire to incorporate their teachers' teachings into their lives. It was not just about knowing what they were saying; it was about being like them. While this approach to discipleship applies to many teachers, teaching, religions, and philosophies today, it does not quite fit when it comes to biblical Christianity. The big difference between our belief and other beliefs of the world is that we believe our founder, Jesus, to be God. While the rest of the world treats Christians as people that follow the 2000-year-old teachings of a man named Jesus, we know them to be the teachings of God Himself, through Jesus who was God in the flesh. This belief makes the discipleship formula "Follow me, listen to my teachings, and be like me" a little more difficult, if not impossible, especially the "be like me" part. This is where the Gospel or the good news of salvation comes in. We must be saved before we can become a follower who learns from Christ to be like Him. Not only did Jesus tell us to follow Him, He provided a way for us through salvation to do this.

The Roman Road, Four Spiritual Laws, Steps to Peace with God—all share the same remarkable message about how to become a follower of Jesus. It's simply that God loves us, desires a relationship with us, and, through the sacrifice of His Son, Jesus Christ, has provided forgiveness for all the sins that separate us from Himself. Through faith and surrender, we can experience this relationship and become followers of Jesus and His teachings.

When Christians talk about salvation, they are often referring to what they see as a single act of God. "One day I surrendered my life to Christ and He saved me" is often all that is meant by salvation. But the message of salvation in the Bible is much more. In the Bible, salvation may be referring to one of three aspects. It may be talking about God's present, potential, or future act of salvation. To understand this, we need to understand three theological terms that describe salvation holistically. These terms are *regeneration, sanctification*, and *glorification*. Not only do we need to understand these terms, we also need to understand how the stories they create can be used to connect with others to help bring them to Christ. As the Holy Spirit works in the life of others, we need to be prepared with the appropriate salvation message that meets them where they are.

Unlike the Ronco Veg-O-Matic, I am not dicing up salvation into three separate parts, nor am I blending it until the elements lose their distinctiveness. These three are all important parts of the whole but realized at different times in different ways. In regeneration we actually get the whole gift of salvation, but like any gift, it must be unwrapped and used to be experienced in its fullness. In regeneration we are made new in Christ with the potential of abundant life (sanctification) and the promise of heaven (glorification).

## *Story of Past Regeneration: I Have Been Saved from the Penalty of Sin*

*Romans 5:1-2 (NLT) Therefore, since we have been made right in God's sight by faith, we have peace with God because of what Jesus Christ our Lord has done for us. 2 Because of our faith, Christ has brought us into this place of undeserved privilege where we now stand, and we confidently and joyfully look forward to sharing God's glory.*

Being saved or becoming a Christian is more an act of surrender than commitment; it's more a need for peace than establishing a new alliance. When a person experiences salvation, he does not commit his small forces to God's superior army. We do not join God as an ally with His kingdom; we surrender as an enemy of His Kingdom. Paul writes to the church of Ephesians describing life before Christ.

*Ephesians 2:1-3 As for you, you were dead in your transgressions and sins, ² in which you used to live when you followed the ways of this world and of the ruler of the kingdom of the air, the spirit who is now at work in those who are disobedient. ³ All of us also lived among them at one time, gratifying the cravings of our flesh and following its desires and thoughts. Like the rest, we were by nature deserving of wrath.*

Dead in sin, followers of the behaviors of the world, under the rule of Satan who lives to disobey God, living to satisfy the desires of our fallen nature: all of this puts us at odds with God and in the place of enemies. Like rebellious terrorists out to destroy God and all He created, we are under the wrath of the Creator. We need peace with God that can be experienced only through our total surrender, peace that can be experienced only through forgiveness, and peace that can be ours only as we lay down all weapons of war and bow,

> **Like rebellious terrorists out to destroy God and all He created, we are under the wrath of the Creator.**

pleading for mercy, before the overwhelming forces. The good news is peace is a prayer away because amnesty is already provided for all who surrender to God. Paul puts it this way.

*Ephesians 2: 4-5 (NIV) But because of his great love for us, God, who is rich in mercy, ⁵ made us alive with Christ even when we were dead in transgressions—it is by grace you have been saved*

Regeneration is the work of God in the life of an individual that changes them from darkness to light. It is the establishment of peace between God and a person, making an enemy of God into a friend of God. It is God's gracious work that secures my eternal soul for heaven and gives me the potential for abundant life on earth. It is the act of God making me a new creation in Christ. It happens the moment one surrenders to the finishing work of Christ, *who died once for sin, the righteous for the unrighteous, to bring us to God* (1 Peter 3:18). In that one instant, God changes a person from being spiritually dead in sin to being spiritually alive in Christ (Eph. 2).

This aspect of salvation is very appealing for those who have suffered as a result of their personal sin. People who have lived in the world influenced by sin for a long time are often influenced by that world. They do not just make wrong choices—they may continually make the wrong choices, developing bad habits that are self-destructive behaviors. They have, as Paul said, made choices to which now they have become slaves. This slavery takes the form of bad habits and addictive practices. Often, what started in secret is now obvious to them and everyone else. These individuals often just want relief, and, like a drowning man, they do not need to be told they are drowning in sin; they just need a life preserver. Throughout my ministry, I have had the opportunity to work with many addicted people and can tell you that most do not need much convincing that sin is real and destructive. Regeneration, forgiveness, a new beginning, a fresh start, and a new creation in Christ are messages that they are ready to hear. The nearness of King Jesus and the salvation from the penalty of sin is the message that gets their attention.

### *Story of Future Glorification: I Will Be Saved from the Presence of Sin*

I remember, as a new believer, hearing the dramatic stories of those who, like the prodigal son of Luke 15, had been living, sleeping, and even eating with the pigs. These conversion stories were so dramatic in comparison to my nine-year-old conversion experience that they would often cause me to doubt it. I later realized that my story was not inadequate but just different from theirs, and, as a pretty good nine-year-old, God's regenerative work in me was just as real inwardly, but the manifestation of it outwardly was less obvious. Upon understanding this, I could better understand

> While in regeneration my place in heaven is secured, in glorification the promise becomes a reality

and appreciate their change from darkness to light. While for some this promise of new life in Christ that leads from darkness to light captures their attention, for me, being a good kid, it did not get mine. What got my attention was the message of heaven or hell. I did not know it as glorification, but the idea of one day having heaven and avoiding hell was appealing to me. It opened up the door for me to understand that sin that would stop me from getting to heaven and that I needed to surrender my life to Jesus. But the truth was I wanted to go to heaven, not hell, and was willing to do or surrender to whatever or whoever would get me there.

While in regeneration my place in heaven is secured, in glorification the promise becomes a reality. Heaven is my home without the distraction of sin and its consequences. In regeneration we are given the deed to the house; in glorification we are moved in. While regeneration is peace secured, glorification is peace realized. Glorification is at the center of Jesus' promise He made to His disciples to calm their fears about the future.

*John 14:1-3 "Do not let your hearts be troubled. You believe in God; believe also in me. ² My Father's house has many rooms; if that were not so, would I have told you that I am going there to prepare a place for you? ³ And if I go and prepare a place for you, I will come back and take you to be with me that you also may be where I am.*

Glorification is where Christ, either through death or His second coming, takes us to the place He has prepared. In glorification we are saved from the presence of sin and given our home in heaven. Glorification is the finished work of salvation in the life of all true followers of Jesus. The message of salvation is not complete without the promise of heaven. If all we had to look forward to was found in this life, being a Christian would be much less appealing. Thankfully, we have the appeal of a home in heaven free from all sin and consequences. No matter how bad life on earth becomes, no matter how appalling people are toward us, we always have a better life to look forward to. They can kill you, cut you up into little pieces, cook you in a stew, and eat you for lunch, but if you're a Christian, to be absent from this body is to be present with God.

For many years, this message of heaven or glorification was one of the most appealing messages of the church, especially in impoverished areas and times. Throughout history and in many areas of the world today where survival is hard and people toil daily for just enough to survive, salvation from the effects of sin can be very appealing. Many of our old hymns with their emphasis on heaven and the life to come were birthed in difficult times. I am not advocating that we should not do everything we can to alleviate and even eliminate poverty, for we should. I am saying that the promise of heaven is appealing in such situations of life. Death for a Christian who has this hope of heaven is just changing addresses, not that they are ready to call a realtor today. Many people, including myself, became Christians because we wanted to avoid hell and go to heaven.

In addition, the older I get, the more I find the promise of heaven an appealing message. Although I am a healthy 57-year-old, the aches and pains of getting older make the idea of heaven more appealing to me than it was when I was younger. I now better understand the prayer of a family, "Father, please take them home to be with you," as they sit beside the deathbed of a Christian loved one. Remember that every person Jesus healed while He was on earth eventually died. It would have been cruel for Him to raise a dead person to live here on earth forever. Such healing was an opportunity to believe and experience both abundant life on earth and eternal life in heaven.

## *Stories of Present Sanctification: I Am Being Saved from the Power of Sin*

Although it is true that life is better on the other side, in heaven, most people in more affluent areas are too comfortable and shortsighted for this to be an appeal to them. For many, including myself, the idea that God created me to live as though waiting in the airport for the departure to heaven has little appeal. On the other hand, salvation from the power of sin, producing a better quality of life, is appealing. Note the appealing words of Jesus, *The thief comes only to steal and kill and destroy; I have come that they may have life, and have it to the full. (John 10:10 NIV)*

If regeneration is receiving the deed and glorification is taking possession, then sanctification is our preparation for the move. To prepare for the move, we must get rid of the things we do not need and procure the things we do need. In regeneration I am saved from the penalty of sin, and in glorification I will be saved from the presence of sin, but in sanctification I am being saved from the power of sin that is in me and all around me. While regeneration is an instantaneous act performed by God in the heart of the surrendered, sanctification is the ongoing work of God making us holy like He is holy (1 Peter 1:16).

> *If regeneration is receiving the deed and glorification is taking possession, then sanctification is our preparation for the move.*

Like a soldier experiencing posttraumatic syndrome, who you can take out of the battle but may not be able to take the battle out of him, Christians may have peace with God but not experience it fully because of habits carried over from their old life. Sanctification is the journey and the process of living in the peace of God. This is the work of salvation that Paul describes to the church at Philippi.

*Philippians 2:12 (NIV) Therefore, my dear friends, as you have always obeyed—not only in my presence, but now much more in my absence—continue to work out your salvation with fear and trembling,*

Notice Paul says that we should WORK OUT our salvation, not WORK ON it. We work out our salvation because we already possess it. Salvation from the power of sin that is given to us at regeneration must be developed. Like the gift of a tool at Christmas, it must be opened and used to the point of proficiency before its value can be fully appreciated.

I use every honey-do job as an excuse to buy another tool. "Yes, dear, I will do that, but I will need a special tool to get it done." Now I did it; my wife (the editor) is onto me. As I look at the tools in my garage, I find I am proficient with some while with others I may be risking my life to use them. I think the only thing I could do with my welder is burn out my eyes. The point is that just because you own it does not mean you can use it. God, at the point of salvation, has given you all the tools you need to live the abundant life; sanctification is about using them proficiently. We have God's Word, God's Spirit, and God's people. Now we must use these tools to "work out our salvation," becoming rebuilt, changed, transformed, and more like Jesus. As Paul says, *For we are God's handiwork, created in Christ Jesus to do good works, which God prepared in advance for us to do. Ephesians 2:10 (NIV)*

Today, I believe sanctification stories can be one of the best selling points of the church. I have found that the benefits of living a life free from sin and its influence has a tremendous appeal to most people. For many, the journey of being a Christian can be as appealing as the destination. For example, marriage ceremonies all over the world start with the aspirations found in the biblical definition of love of 1 Corinthian 13: 4-7 (NIV).

*4 Love is patient and kind. Love is not jealous or boastful or proud 5 or rude. It does not demand its own way. It is not irritable, and it keeps no record of being wronged. 6 It does not rejoice about injustice but rejoices whenever the truth wins out. 7 Love never gives up, never loses faith, is always hopeful, and endures through every circumstance.*

While these marriages seem to start with the desire to have this kind of love, most are shipwrecked in divorce court by their inability to attain it. How can sanctification stories help? What if there could be a greater chance the couple could have the kind of love they wanted? This is why I stopped counseling the way I traditionally did premarital counseling. Instead of just reading books prior to the wedding and attempting to dialogue with the couple about their future while they are consumed by the wedding, I decided to use the time in our counseling sessions to develop a one-year marriage covenant. This covenant would be designed to create a marriage work ethic that would include the couple engaging healthy married couples and spiritual leaders who would model for them good marriages and hold them accountable for theirs. As my wife and I have engaged this process with newlyweds, we have found opportunity after opportunity to share our sanctification stories about the power of God in our marriage. This honest, open dialogue about issues produced by sin in our marriage (most of them mine) from which God has delivered us is often the catalyst for the couple to evaluate themselves both as individuals and as a couple. Karen and I can comfort with the comfort we have been given and promote reconciliation in the way we have been reconciled as we share our stories of sanctification.

In addition, when you place the desires of our sinful nature next to the fruit produced by the Spirit of God found in Galatians 5:19-23 (NIV), most people would acknowledge a desire for these fruits of the Spirit.

*19 When you follow the desires of your sinful nature, the results are very clear: sexual immorality, impurity, lustful pleasures, 20 idolatry, sorcery, hostility, quarreling, jealousy, outbursts of anger, selfish ambition, dissension, division, 21 envy, drunkenness, wild parties, and other sins like these. Let me tell you again, as I have before, that anyone living that sort of life will not inherit the Kingdom of God. 22 But the Holy Spirit produces this kind of fruit in our lives: love, joy, peace, patience, kindness, goodness, faithfulness, 23 gentleness, and self-control. There is no law against these things!*

When Paul uses the term "sinful nature," he means that it is wrong and natural. It does not take much effort at all to live like the first list in verses 19-21, while the second list in verses 22-23 comes from another source working within us, the Holy Spirit. The question is not if people want this second list, because most do. The question for many is, "How can I get it?" Many people will be receptive if they can see an avenue for attaining the love of 1 Corinthian 13 and the Fruit of the Spirit from Galatians 5. This is the attractional nature of sanctification stories.

Christians for years have been trained to give their testimony, which usually means articulating a story of regeneration or the time in life that he accepted Christ. Although this is important and should be done, it is not the message that is fitting for every person. The message and motives of a nine-year-old salvation story do not always relate to an adult. It is not always the best fit. In addition, while we should also promote the benefit of heaven and one day being saved from the presence of sin, the comfortable shortsighted person may not respond to it because it seems so far away. While all of these stories are good, what may be missing are the ongoing stories of sanctification.

Like my personal conversion story and my belief that heaven is my home, these personal stories of triumph over sin that come from the power of the presence of God are hard for others to deny. In addition, the stories about the power of God at work in our everyday life will often contrast with the spiritual impotence of others and open the door for future conversations.

I was once talking to a lost friend who had a teenage son somewhat younger than mine. As he was sharing his struggles about raising a teenage boy who at times could be rebellious, he asked me for my advice. I then told him the following story about my struggle.

*There was a time when I felt the way you did and went to two men I really trusted and asked their advice as you are asking for mine. Both of these men told me that if they could do it all again, they would be more patient with their sons when they were teenagers. Upon hearing what I felt to be wise counsel, I begin regularly praying for patience, not the kind learned by endurance and struggles, but the special endowment God promises when we surrender to Him. It was not long after this that I noticed God beginning to answer my prayer and to change me. When my son did something dumb or rebellious, I noticed I did not feel the pressing need to nip it in the bud, and things that I would have reacted or over reacted to, I would just let run their course and allow him to suffer the consequences for his own actions. What I found is that the consequences that I was trying to prevent through angry confrontation were teaching him more than I ever could. In fact, on many occasions after experiencing the consequences, he would debrief with me and allow me to offer my advice. The patience that God gave me greatly improved my relationship with my son.*

In telling this story, I identified with my friend's struggle and anger, which formed a connection with him. With this connection I was able to share with him about the active, present power of God in my life. This testimony of God's power in my life stood in contrast to the powerlessness of his life without Christ and opened the door for me to share more of my faith with him.

This is the power of sanctification stories. Stories of God saving us from the power of sin are both imminent and transcendent. Imminent means close points of connection and that we identify with the real problems of real people. Imminent means we understand what they did, why they did it, and how they feel about it now.

The present tense stories of God's power are also transcendent. This means they are stories that rise above the problems with solutions that come from God's presence within us. Like the story of regeneration that began with, "I am a sinner (generally)," these stories begin with "I have a sin (specifically)." Like the regeneration story where God delivers us from hell and the consequences of our sins and gives us heaven as a free gift, sanctification stories are about God's deliverance from our individual hellish habits into a life more abundant.

People do not just need to know that you have been saved from the penalty of sin. They do not just need to know that you will be saved from the presence of sin. They do need to know that you are being saved from the power of sin. They need to know that you have experienced the fullness of God's salvation and that they can, too.

## THE SANCTIFICATION STORIES MUST START WITH YOU

The real starting place for **finding** the person OF peace is **being** a person AT peace with God. Jesus assumes you are a person experiencing peace when He says, "If the person of peace be there, YOUR peace will rest on him." You cannot give away what you do not possess first. My wife is so smart, probably because she reads a lot. Well, I'm smart, too, because I listen to what she's reading and don't have to read it myself. She once told me of an article that stated it was wrong to force children to share. As good Christians, we have all learned the importance of sharing from a very young age. Most of us, after giving our children toys on their birthdays, would strongly encourage them to share them with friends and family, reinforcing the idea of sharing. Isn't this a good thing? Well, according to this article, maybe not. Forcing our children to share before they have a sense of ownership may not be teaching them to share it all because children must learn ownership before they can learn sharing. Forcing a child to share before they have a sense of ownership may be teaching them that the gift you gave was really community property. In the same way, you and I cannot really share something we do not own. We cannot share a public park or a public swimming pool because they are not ours to share. We can share in them, but we are really not sharing them.

Today, many Christians, if they share at all, are just sharing community property. They do not share Christ and His great power over sin because they do not own it. Church for many is like the public pool or park; they share in it as community without owning it personally. The message they take home is *come and share the experience with me*. Although this is not a bad message, it is dreadfully incomplete. It lacks full ownership of the great gift of salvation that God desires for us to give and that Jesus died for us to own. The secret to sharing it may be possessing it. Until we experience the ownership of salvation in its fullest sense, we will not share it. Without experiencing the assurance of regeneration, the hope of glorification, and the influence of sanctification, we will not have a message fit for the person of peace or the worthy person.

Even though the tools for our journey are free, the journey is not effortless. Sanctification is work. Paul says we are to "work out our salvation with fear and trembling." Like a fireman who cannot work in the midst of a fire without respect (fear and trembling) for it, we cannot work with God, who is an all-consuming fire, without respect for Him and the resources He gives us. Yes, God has given us everything we need to live the life He designed and desired for us, but we must work at proficiency. At this point, I am going to give you a big component for successfully living the Christian life. It is a must—without it you are just playing at or pretending to be a Christian. Although it is simple, it is the real work of Christianity. YOU MUST SURRENDER. Yes, let go, stop, cease, and halt. Sounds easy? It's not. It is the hardest thing you will do as a Christian. You must stop trying to join forces with God; stop thinking you have something to offer that even approaches His power and might. Real Christianity is not an alliance but a forfeit.

Something else to know: you are not a refugee seeking asylum in the war between good and evil, between God and Satan. Again, Ephesians 2 tells us that we were enemies of God. James tells us that friendship with this world is enmity with God. Before Christ, you were the enemy of God and His good plan. Regeneration happened the moment you surrendered as an enemy to the Almighty God. He mercifully forgave you and made you a part of His Kingdom. Even though we have been forgiven and given new life, we have brought a lot of baggage with us—things we think are important for our journey but they're not—things we think are right but they're wrong—good things in the wrong places—right things used unrighteously. The valuables we gathered in darkness are garbage in the light of God. In the new life we been given, everything must be evaluated and much of it must go.

Sanctification is the continual act of surrender. While in one act of surrender to God I was saved from the penalty of sin, it is in the daily acts of surrender that I am saved from the power of sin. In regeneration, we give UP OUR LIFE: in sanctification, we daily give OF OUR LIFE. When I was in prison, as a teacher and chaplain, I learned that the worst punishment that a person could receive was to take their life, via the death penalty, but I also realized that the second worst thing was to take of their life, e.g., a 10-year sentence. To be sentenced to 10, 15, 20 years is taking OF YOUR LIFE. In addition, although I have known many fathers who would give UP THEIR LIFE for their wife and children, I have often found the wife and children complain because these same men are not willing to give OF THEIR LIFE. Follow the analogy. Regeneration is when we surrender our lives up to God while sanctification is surrendering of our lives to God. The real question is: are you living for what you say you would die for?

How do we know sanctification is taking place in our lives? In what ways will we know that we are growing and maturing in Christ? All of these have to be measured on an individual level. Not every person starts at the same place or moves at the same rate. Some have more to overcome than others. I remember a story told about a pastor who led a church in a very rough area. The people he reached grew up with little or no exposure to Christian values. One day, a couple from the Bible Belt visited the church and afterwards met with the pastor. Although they loved the service and preaching, they had one criticism. It seemed that as they were walking into the church, they saw a group outside smoking together; this was ok until they walked in to the church, sat down, and noticed the same group coming on the stage to lead worship. As they explained to the pastor their concerns of having leaders who were setting such a bad example, the pastor stood up and interrupted in a shocked tone, "What were they smoking?" The perplexed couple answered, "Well, cigarettes." The pastor relaxed and said, "Oh, good. You should have seen what these guys used to smoke."

The truth is, and hopefully this illustrates it, that while all are depraved, some people's depravity is much deeper and darker than others'. Sanctification for the young man raised in church may be quite different from sanctification for the one raised on the streets. It has been my experience that as a spiritual blank slate before God, the young man raised on the streets may progress faster than the young man raised in all the traditions of the church. The young man raised in church may need to tear down old ideas about the church and replace them with meaningful ones which may make his journey longer. Spiritual maturity is a continual movement forward in the direction of Christlikeness, but the starting place in the journey of holiness may be quite different for different people. Therefore, we must measure spiritual growth in terms of movement forward. Our success as Christians on this earth should be determined not by perfection but by the idea of being MORE like Jesus.

Although there is movement and progress, there are also stages of development, and one must be significantly completed before the other can begin. I have categorized these two stages as mercy and grace. Mercy refers to the stage of sanctification and discipleship where God is emptying the vessel of impurities while grace refers to the stage where, after removing and cleaning the vessel, God can then fill it with good stuff. Paul's writings to the church of Ephesus depict these stages using the imagery of taking off and putting on clothes.

*Ephesians 4:20-24 That, however, is not the way of life you learned 21 when you heard about Christ and were taught in him in accordance with the truth that is in Jesus. 22 You were taught, with regard to your former way of life, to put off your old self, which is being corrupted by its deceitful desires; 23 to be made new in the attitude of your minds; 24 and to put on the new self, created to be like God in true righteousness and holiness.*

Like taking a shower every day, we must continually take off the old, clean up, and put on the new. The difference is the new is not just cleaner but better, with the cumulative effect of dressing or making me more like Jesus. Sanctification is the continual act of surrender where God empties us of sin, self, and Satan's influence and replaces them with Christlike character. Below are some signs that sanctification is taking place in our lives within these two stages of development.

<u>Mercy</u>
- I have a greater sensitivity to personal sin and its effects on God and others. I feel the pain that God feels when I do things that harm others and myself.
- I have more of a desire for God's will over my personal desires.
- I have fewer desires of the flesh and more for the fruit of the spirit (Galatians 5)
- I am hungry to spend time in God's Word. Although painful at times, I desire to address issues that stand between God and me.
- I am continually challenging my thoughts, attitudes, values, and traditions with God's Word.
- I want to be held accountable by other Christians concerning the changes God is making in my life.
- I seek to replace bad habits in my life with good ones that support my growing love for Him and others.
- I take greater risks produced by faith in God. I am known for going outside my comfort zone.

- I sometimes experience persecution from others, sometimes friends and family, because of the changes God has brought to my life.
- I sometimes find that people notice the changes God has produced in me and want to know more.
- Although I am not perfect, there are no consistent sins in my life that would embarrass Christ and His cause.

<u>Grace</u>
- I have more love for God and others expressed in a desire to serve more sacrificially – 1 Corinthian 13, Matthew 22
- I have a greater desire for spiritual things and internal change expressed in Christ like character.
- I hunger to spend time in God's Word to learn more about God, me, and others, in order to know them better, love them more, and serve them better.
- I want to do more for God and others. I especially want to help others know God better.
- Because I realize all that God has given me, I desire to give back to Him my time, talents, and treasure as a token of appreciation.
- I have a greater sensitivity to lostness in my spheres of influence.
- I grieve over the sins of others as I see them suffering the consequences of their actions. I want them to surrender to the help God offers.

# CHAPTER 15: OVERCOMING FEAR: PREPARE TO BE BITTEN

*Matthew 10:16 (NIV) I am sending you out like sheep among wolves.*

*Luke 10:3 (NIV) Go! I am sending you out like lambs among wolves.*

The person of peace is often found in the midst of adversity, in the midst of wolves. Who likes adversity? I don't. Could you imagine being a sheep having to find other sheep in a pack of wolves? That is scary. Maybe one reason we are not finding the person of peace is because we are afraid of being bitten. If we are going to find the person of peace, we must overcome fear.

> *While most of us would love to be called "the salt of the earth" and "the light to the world," we may not want the opposition from those who prefer low-sodium diets in the darkness.*

Jesus prepared His followers by realistically painting a picture of a plentiful harvest in a pack of wolves. In my previous book, I wrote the following:

*Influence does not mean that everyone will like us; it just means that as God's ambassadors, we will be noticed. Being salt of the earth and light to the world does not mean that some will not prefer the unsalted earth and unlighted world. The bland and blind may hate or even kill those who try to influence them as salt and light.*
*– Transformative Church Planting Movement*

While most of us would love to be called "the salt of the earth" and "the light to the world," we may not want the opposition from those who prefer low-sodium diets in the darkness. If you are going to stand for anything, you must be prepared for those who will stand against you. Jesus spends a great deal of time preparing His disciples for the opposition they will encounter as His followers.

I have heard that two of the greatest fears of most people are the fear of death and the fear of public speaking. I would add to this list a third one—the fear of rejection. Learning to overcome the fear of death may be difficult, but the fear of public speaking and the fear of rejection can be dealt with. While most of us would prefer our fears to be dealt with by a miracle or avoidance, more often they are dealt with through exposure and practice. A commitment to practice is essential to overcoming the fear of rejection, to witnessing, and to finding the person of peace. Knowing whom we should really fear, how love can diminish fears, and a practical process for dealing with fear can help us overcome the fear of rejection.

## PERSON TO FEAR

*Jesus says, "Do not be afraid of those who kill the body but cannot kill the soul. Rather, be afraid of the One who can destroy both soul and body in hell." Matthew 10:28 (NIV)*

It seems like almost every time God showed Himself in a way that gave humanity a taste of His glory, it was met with fear. Fear like, "God, you're awesome. Now please don't destroy me." You would think that the fear of God itself would motivate us to do whatever He told us to do, such as the Great Commission. God, who holds our breath and our eternal destiny in His hand, commanded us to fulfill that. Given God's power to destroy us on earth and for all eternity, you would think there would be no competition as to whom we would choose to fear and follow. Sadly, this is not the case. Most Christians fear the persecution of man more than disobedience to God.

Life is about knowing whom and what to fear. John Stossel once did a show about the risk-taking behavior of young people. A test was given to adults and teenagers measuring brain activity for both groups as they viewed the same set of images. The researchers found that in the adults the reasoning part of the brain was more active while in the teenagers the instinctive and reactionary part of the brain showed more activity. The conclusion was that teenagers are more likely to engage in risky behaviors because of a lack of experience. Most adults fear risky behaviors because we have experienced the pain that resulted from them, but most teenagers lack the experience that produces fear. Most of us would also agree that a healthy sense of fear would save lives, especially among teenagers. Some fear is good.

This is what Jesus is saying in the passage above. In the same way that the fear of death can overshadow the fear of chemotherapy for a patient with cancer, a healthy sense of the fear of God, who holds our eternal souls in His hands, makes all other fears in this life pale in comparison.

Like Dorothy, the Cowardly Lion, the Scarecrow, and the Tin Man in the movie *The Wizard of Oz*, the things we fear are often the smoke and mirrors produced by the small, impotent wizard behind the curtain. As powerful and ominous the CREATURE may appear and as powerful and ominous whatever weapons he may fashion against us appear, it or they can never exceed the power and awe of the CREATOR. While Paul tells us in Ephesians 6 that "we wrestle not against flesh and blood but against principalities, against powers of darkness," he does not tell us to fear them. Instead, he describes a triumphant soldier who has defeated these enemies because he is fully armed with armor supplied by God. Therefore, we should not fear the principalities and powers of darkness, but instead we should fear incomplete armament; we should fear our failure to trust in God and all He has provided for us. *I am sending you as sheep among wolves* is not a warning to fear the wolves but an admonishment to be prepared—prepared not for the fight but for faith in the Good Shepherd who knows and will protect His sheep.

## POWER OF LOVE THAT DEALS WITH FEAR

The more important tool for overcoming fear is love. John tells us that there is no fear in love because "perfect (or mature) love drives out fear" (1 John 4:18). Most of us understand the idea of maturing love that replaces fear as we care for aging parents. As a child, I did what my parents told me to do out of fear of punishment. As a young teenager and young adult, still in many ways dependent on them, I did what they asked partly because I feared losing support. I always loved my parents and knew that they loved me, but fear was always a part of my motivation during those early years. As I moved away and became more independent, my motives changed. As I had my own family and could identify more with my parents, I grew in my understanding and appreciation for them. Now, we do whatever we can to help them, whatever they ask or tell us to do; we do it in their way and in their time, not for fear that they will discipline us if we don't do it, but because we love them. As I think about this illustration, I must ask, "What really changed?" Well, I did. I grew up. As an adult I understood that most of the rules I rebelled against were created for me and my protection. As a parent I understood the great sacrifices that parents make for their children. This knowledge and perspective changed the way I thought and felt about my parents. Sacrifices that I once denied I now valued. Advice I once ignored I now invited and appreciated. Out of a deep sense of gratitude for all my parents did for me, I now wanted to do for them. Why? Because I love them. My point is this: love can replace fear and be a much more powerful motivator for service than fear is. From a parent's perspective, no healthy parent wants their adult children to serve them out of fear. No, we want them to serve us because they love us, and if I have done things right as a parent, they will. If we have produced mature children, they will relate to us more as friends than children, and out of this mature, loving relationship, they will help us in our time of need.

> *Only those completely detached from emotions would be fearless, and this is neither natural nor healthy.*

Just like love replaces fear in our relationship with our parents, it can also replace my fear of sharing my faith with my friends and neighbors. As I spend time with my neighbors, and as we talk together, I grow in my understanding of them. As we share stories of our lives, we find points at which our understanding turns to intimacy. After a while, my fear of rejection is overcome by my love for them and my desire to see them experience a relationship with God. When I really know my neighbors, I grow to love them; the more that I love and care about them, the more I want them to know God. My fear of witnessing and possible rejection is replaced by my loving desire to see my friends benefit from a relationship with God. Out of my love for them, I want my friends to know my friend—Jesus Christ.

## PROCESS FOR DEALING WITH FEAR

You can learn how to deal with fear. The real answer to fear is not fearlessness but courage. What we might refer to as fearless actions—the life-saving acts of soldiers, police, fire fighters, and others—are really acts of courage. Only those completely detached from emotions would be fearless, and this is neither natural nor healthy. Psychopaths and sociopaths are unhealthy people without conscience or emotions, who do not fear the law, the authorities, or God. For most of us, fear is not voluntary but an involuntary response to a threat. When faced with a threat, fear is the natural stimulus that kicks in our fight or flight response. Courage is a choice I make in spite of those feelings. Courage is the thing that causes heroes to run toward threats while everyone else runs away. Courage is what causes the police officer to move toward an armed criminal when everyone else moves in the opposite direction. Courage is what causes a fire fighter to go into a burning building when everyone else is scrambling to get out. It was courage, a choice made in spite of fear, that caused the crew and passengers on United Airlines Flight 93 to fight back on 9/11 against their terrorist hijackers, preventing their plane from crashing into Washington, D.C. They were not fearless—they were courageous.

Some heroes are spontaneously birthed from a courageous response to a threat while others are trained to respond. Be it spontaneous or a product of training, both face their fears with heroic courage. Therefore, fear can be overcome with training. Most training takes the similar course of *knowledge* that leads to *perspective*, that leads to *conviction, competence* and *character*.

When I started as a teacher in the Federal Bureau of Prisons, my only formal teaching experience was my student teaching some 10 years prior. So starting this new job, motivated by the fear of failure, I got my hands on every piece of information I could. I brought home educational manuals, teaching books, and policy handbooks so I could pore over them on my own time. The more I knew about the FBP, my institution, and my job, the less I feared the unknown. The more I got into the information, the more the information got into me and changed my perspective. Although still inexperienced in my job, I began to see it and me more clearly. I could see my ability to do this job. Out of this perspective came the conviction that I could do this job. With this conviction came the desire to do a good job, which led to competence. The more I did, the more I felt comfortable being called a teacher. As a teacher, I then felt confident acquiring more knowledge, a greater perspective, more conviction, and greater proficiency. In the span of a year, I moved from a novice to an experienced teacher to the Literacy Coordinator and was in line for an associate department-head job. In addition, I surpassed many of the education goals set by our regional administration and was recognized by the warden, associate warden, and others for my accomplishment. What you do not know about this story is that I was a horrible academic who hated most of my school career, and I became a teacher because it was the shortest distance to seminary. In addition, I took this job as a teacher to feed my family after burning out and leaving the ministry. I was not just afraid of this job; I was afraid I could not do any job. It stood as a test of my ability to provide as a man for my family. In one year, God took a burned-out church-planting pastor and turned him into a successful teacher for the Federal Bureau of Prisons. God conquered my fears using knowledge to show me I was not stupid, perspective to help me see that I could do the job, conviction to motivate me to do it well, competence that earned me right to be called a teacher, and influence that made me a Christian teacher.

I have moved my family all over Texas on to California and then to Ohio for different ministry assignments. Somewhere between the accepting of the ministry assignments and the actually deployment, some nights, certainly more than one, I would wake up in a cold sweat with an overwhelming sense of fear, saying to myself, "What am I doing? I have never done anything like this before? Why am I doing this?" I battled this fear with prayer to the God who called me. I trusted that, just as the landowner in the Parable of the Talents gave to his servants, God has given to me according my abilities. I remembered the time God sent me to prison and, through the process of knowledge, perspective, conviction, competence and character, gave me courage to conquer my fears.

> *While we proclaim, it is the Spirit that reclaims the soul of a person.*

Many fears, such as the fear of rejection, are unrealistic fears. Our minds, coupled with Satan's schemes, can create fears that are more fantasy than reality. Knowledge can help dispel these fears. Spending time with others and gathering information about them can lead to strategies for encounters. When your neighbor tells you that they or a family member is sick, it is easy to imagine yourself offering to pray for them the next time you see them. The more I know my neighbors, the more likely I am to know what the outcome of a conversation about Jesus will produce. The more time you spend with them, the more you know them and the more you can identify with them. The common ground of experience helps you to see things from their perspective. Like the incarnate Christ, God in the flesh, you can now see them as God sees them and as they see themselves. But just like Christ, who sees from God's and man's perspective, hanging out and getting to know them will eventually provoke feelings in us. Jesus modeled this for us.

*Matthew 9: 35-36 Jesus went through all the towns and villages, teaching in their synagogues, proclaiming the good news of the kingdom and healing every disease and sickness. 36 When he saw the crowds, he had compassion on them, because they were harassed and helpless, like sheep without a shepherd.*

Just like the compassion of Jesus, the more we spend time with people, the more we see and the more we feel compassion for them. It is at the pivot point of feelings that we decide to do something; being moved by compassion, we must move with compassion. This love expressed in compassion pushes away our fear of rejection so that we must share.

# CHAPTER 16: TOOLS TO HELP DISCOVER THE PERSON OF PEACE

## USING TOOLS PROFICIENTLY

Tools are good, but tools are useless and even dangerous without competence. Competence is the difference between smashing your thumb with a hammer or building a house with it. In the same way, tools for sharing our faith are best used by the competent. By competence I mean a person who knows his tools so well that when they are used, they become an extension of that person. Like the tools a woodworker uses as he works a lathe or a sculptor uses as he works on a sculpture, a proficient discipler knows how and when to apply the tools they have been trained to use.

Effective evangelism can never be produced by a checklist of knowledge alone. While we inform, it is the Spirit that transforms. While we proclaim, it is the Spirit that reclaims the soul of a person. The Spirit must become an intuitive part of our being. Responding to the work of the Holy Spirit must become innate, natural, or part of the character of the sharer. This is built through the process of knowledge, perspective, conviction, competence, and character. Most evangelical Christians know they should be witnesses, yet the vast majority never share their faith. Although knowing the command to make disciples and be a witness is important, it seems the importance does not penetrate any further than information. They know what God knows but do not see lostness the way He sees it. Thus, the need for perspective. Perspective happens when knowledge becomes personal, when I see the lostness of humanity in the face of someone I love. Jesus did not just know people were lost; He saw fields ripe unto harvest and saw harassed sheep without a shepherd.

In addition to this, Jesus' perspective drove Him to feeling. He wept over the lostness and rebellion of His people. He had compassion for the harassed, lost sheep. Like Jesus' knowledge became perspective and then conviction, so must our knowledge of lostness move us to perspective and then to conviction. Conviction is the pivot point between knowing and doing. We will not witness or have the character of a witness for Christ until we know what He knows about lostness, see it the way He sees it, and feel about it the way He feels about it. When deep conviction takes root, something must be done about what we know and see; thus, conviction leads to competence. Competence is the development of proficiency that comes from doing something based on good knowledge, healthy perspective, and passionate convictions. We are witnesses when we witness not just because we know we should, see the need, or feel the urge. On the other hand, when witnessing is a product of competence, motivated by strong conviction, influenced by a powerful perspective, and based upon appropriate knowledge, we can lay claim to the character of being a witness.

## UNDERSTANDING THE JOURNEY OF SALVATION

What does the journey from lostness to salvation to ministry/mission look like? This is a question that many evangelists and seminary professors have attempted to quantify. One tool used in many Christian schools, seminaries, and churches was produced by James F. Engel and is called the Engel's Scale of Evangelism (See Below).

### Engel's Scale of Evangelism

+10 Openness to others/Effective sharing of faith and
+9 Prayer
+8 Stewardship of resources
+7 Christian life-style
+6 Discovery and use of gifts
+5 Growth in Christian character
+4 Growth in understanding of the faith
+3 Become part of the process of making other disciples
+2 Initiation into the church
+1 Evaluation of decision
0 A Disciple is born!
-1 Repentance and faith
-2 Challenge and decision to act
-3 Awareness of personal need
-4 Positive attitude to the Gospel
-5 Grasp of implications of the Gospel
-6 Awareness of basic facts of the Gospel
-7 Interest in Christianity
-8 Initial Awareness of Christianity
-9 No effective knowledge of Christianity
-10 Awareness of the supernatural

As you become aware of people, Engel's Scale can help you identify, pray, and engage them more effectively. For example, if they are completely unaware of Christianity, you may be the person God uses to bring them to a basic understanding of the Gospel. Where this really helps is in understanding that moving someone from lostness to salvation to fruitfulness is often just moving them from one step to another. You could literally place beside the name of each individual the appropriate number that best describes where you feel they are spiritually.

I used to have a reputation in my family that I know I got from my father. I was the person that Jack Nicholson referred to in the movie *A Few Good Men* when he said, "You can't handle the truth." No! I had a hard time handling the truth **about me**. When confronted with the truth concerning my character, I would get defensive, resist, and argue about it (often proving their point for coming to me in the first place), but once I got away from the situation and the emotions subsided, I would consider this truth. Often, given time to think, I would come back to the table admitting it as truth, often with an apology about how I handled it in the first place. I later realized that this process exhausted my wife and raised the stress level of my family. Today Karen would testify that I (by the grace of God) have gotten better at handling the truth and that I am better at listening and less defensive (but still a work in progress).

I think the changes that I have made are a result of the people I have pastorally counseled who are just like me. Getting them to consider a truth that would lead to the betterment of their life and their marriage was like swimming upstream. The slightest progress was a lot of work for me. While most people are not as outwardly defiant or defensive as I was, most people do need time to process truth. This is important because having time to contemplate truth can change it from general truth to MY TRUTH, and until truth about an individual is owned by that individual, nothing changes. This is where tools like Engel's Scale are helpful. Knowing these steps can help us to know where an individual is and what truth we need to give them to help move them to the next step. Persons of peace may be at different levels on this scale, with the pattern of processing looking something like this: I approach, they are receptive; I present the truth, they process, accept it, and become receptive to the next level; I present the truth, they process and accept and so on and so forth. The person of peace may be receptive to the whole process all at once or to sections of it or to individual steps. One thing that is important to remember is that receptivity is like a switch that can be turned on or off, and people can become receptive and unreceptive at any level. As you encounter a person that seems to have stopped, they may need time to process. When this occurs, pray for them and continue to test for receptivity.

This scale can be used to map an individual's progress or a group's progress. It could also be used to work with individuals to form groups around common areas of spiritual need. Engel's scale may be more important in the U.S. than the mission field because, while many groups encountered by missionaries probably start at the same place, groups in America could be spiritually diverse. The people we encounter in our work place, home place, or play place may range from the refugee who is completely unaware of Christ to the Christian who is discovering his spiritual gifts. What I have found is that, in general, when you put Christians together with lost people to study the Bible, the lost people will clam up. When you put people in the upper level of Engel's Scale with those in the lower levels, those in the upper level will unintentionally dominate the conversation and sometimes sound preachery to others not on their level. On the other hand, grouping individuals of similar spiritual journeys will encourage them to share without embarrassment. The exception to this would be mixing individuals for leadership training.

## SERVE OTHERS

Jesus said He did not come to be served but to serve (Mk 10:45). Serving others is the atmosphere for meeting the person of peace. For years we have used Maslow's Hierarchy of Needs in our evangelism efforts. We strive to meet the basic needs of individuals in hopes of meeting their greatest need for Jesus. We feed the body to alleviate the obstacle of hunger so that we may offer them the Bread of Life. Meeting social needs has always been at the heart of the ministry of the church. We do not do it conditionally to force belief; we do it unconditionally to offer the opportunity to believe. Jesus modeled meeting the physical needs of people by healing them, feeding them, and loving them unconditionally, but He always did it to show them He was God in the flesh and to offer them the hope of salvation.

While coaching gymnastics, I had a rule: "Offer to all equally. To those who take, give more." There were many reasons kids came to gym. Some came because mom made them while others desired to learn the skills. It was not long before I would know who was there because they wanted to be there. It was a joy to work with the willing souls, and it was work to work with the others. While I always offered an opportunity to all to learn something, I consistently found myself working more with the ones who enjoyed being there. Likewise, Jesus offered to all equally, but to those who accepted from Him, He gave more. It was to His disciples who chose to be there that He entrusted the meaning behind His parables. While we should continually offer to all, it is natural to spend more time with the ones who want to know more, see more, do more, and be more.

One caution I would offer in using this tool is that it should be used to support and not enable. I have found that one of the great struggles of being a parent is the desire to support without enabling. I want to help my children without creating an attitude of entitlement. While Jesus was always supportive and loving, He was never enabling. While we could look at the needs of people as an avenue to the Gospel, it can also be a hindrance. In John 6, Jesus works with a group of people who have experienced God's miracle of feeding, but they cannot seem to move beyond their need of food to see the real Bread of life.

If meeting needs becomes an end in itself instead of the means to the Gospel, we have created a social Gospel. Imagine with me if all the problems of the world were solved, with no more wars, famine, hunger, sickness, or disease. The world would be a great place to live, but what then? What about life after death? If God created man with an immortal soul that will go on after this life, would it not be sad to have 100 years of a great life and spend eternity in hell? Better a little hell on earth with God than eternal life in hell without Him. It was good that every person Jesus healed or raised from the dead eventually died. Resurrection and healing for them was never an end in itself but an opportunity and means to meet the greater need of knowing God.

## MAPPING YOUR MISSIONAL ENVIRONMENTS

The best place to plant seeds are in the fields of your life, the environments that God has already placed you in. My missional environment is the place and people groups of my potential influence where through the Holy Spirit I will make followers, learners, and influencers for Christ. It is my God-given field to cultivate, plant, water, weed, and harvest. These environments could include home, work, school, and recreational settings.

> ...stop anticipating the mission field and planning for it and realize you are already there.

In order for this to work, you must live a life that demonstrates you are convinced that God is sovereign. That means large and in charge and that He has a purpose for your life and a schedule for your day. You must be surrendered to the divine places and appointments He has set for you. You must stop anticipating and planning for the mission field and realize you are already there. The world we live in is filled with people who need Christ. Specifically, the world YOU live in is filled with people whom Christ loved so much that He died for them. These lost people are not out there; they are right here, next to you. They are not just the unreached people groups of the 20/40 window. They are the unreached people you call your neighbors, your coworkers, your friends, and even your family. It is time you realized that God did not give you a home, job, or gym membership so you can live, work, and have fun. NO, God has given you a home place, work place, and play place to be an ambassador and missionary for Him.

Once again, we must realize the Holy Spirit is always at work preparing me for people and preparing people for me. The God who has changed your life and given you a message is also preparing others to observe your life and engage your message.

Mapping your missional environment will help you evaluate receptivity in your present settings and discover "persons of peace." It will help you pray more specifically and effectively, cultivating for future influence. In addition, it will make you more aware of and sensitive to the work of the Holy Spirit and the opportunities God is presenting.

You need to be prepared that receptivity may fall in one of these three areas: Gospel, grow or go. Gospel means that this person is in need of and receptive to becoming a follower of Christ. Grow refers to the person who has accepted Christ, sometimes years before, and is receptive to reading, knowing, and growing in Christ. The third group, and one I seem to work a lot with, consists of individuals who know Christ and have grown in Christ but have never been challenged to Go. These are individuals who have experienced God, who understand their need to be influencers for Christ, and who are receptive to being a missionary in their home place, work place, and play place.

*How to Map Your Missional Environment*

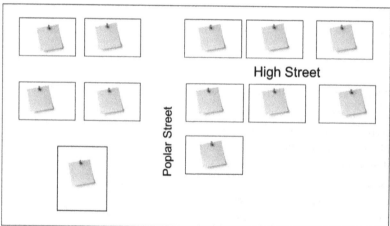

On a poster board or butcher paper, draw your home place, work place, or play place. Let's use your home place as an example. For each home that surrounds yours, put a box big enough to write in or place post-it notes. In these boxes or on the post-it notes, write down names and everything you know about the people in each home. Write down prayer concerns including physical, emotional, financial needs. If you don't have anything to write in these areas, you probably do not know your neighbors.

If you have nothing to write, start by asking for prayer concerns. As a minister, I must say of the thousands of times I have asked someone if I could pray for them, there have been many times that it was met with surprise and perplexity, but I can count on one hand the number of times that someone was offended by it. 99.9% of the time, even asking specific questions like, "How can I pray for you today?" has been met with openness, honesty, and appreciation. Statistics tell us that most people do not have a problem with God, Jesus, or prayer—just Christians and church. Asking someone how you can pray for them starts your relationship with them with you being identified as a caring Christian. While some may train you to build a relationship with others before you define yourself as a Christian, I would encourage you to let them know your affiliation with Christ early in your relationship because the more invested you become in the relationship, the greater the cost if rejected. In other words, the deeper the friendship becomes before you identify yourself as a Christian, the less likely you may be to risk it. Nonetheless, we should always be willing to sacrifice our relationship with them for their relationship with God and His truth.

As a man, I can engage another man in 15 minutes of conversation and know his profession, hobbies, and interests, and he mine. Why? Because this is a major part who he is. If this is true, then to delay in letting someone know you are caring Christian may appear to minimize your relationship with Christ. Asking how you can pray them is often a pleasant surprise for a person and essential to the encounter. At this point, I need to remind you that I am not talking about a witnessing strategy; I am talking about calling on the God of this universe to help you and to intervene in their lives. Prayer is not practice and preparation for the game: it is the game. You must sincerely believe that God is at work and that prayer is His way for you to engage that work in the lives of your neighbors, with you wanting to know about them so you can know them. Prayer does not put God in our setting. It propels us into His. However, don't dial the number if you do not expect an answer. Also, remember to write the prayer requests down. This will keep them fresh in your mind and be a continual reason to engage them in conversation. I have some neighbors who are lost that have a great respect for me and will even voluntarily approach me with prayer concerns.

For clarification, your home place may be the families in the neighborhood of the home you own or the apartments around the one you are renting. Your work place could be the departments at your job or the cubicles around your workstation. Your play place could be the people that you regularly encounter as you work out, coach, or participate on a team. Your play place might include clubs you are a member of as you golf, exercise, or ride your bike. Whatever you are doing, God has not given you these things as an end in themselves to satisfy your desires; He has given them to you as environments to impact for His Kingdom. The truth is you are already on the mission field—you are already an ambassador. The question is, "Are you the only one who knows you are an ambassador?"

Cautions: Much of what people may share with you is confidential and should not be displayed in public view. Not everyone will understand what you are doing. While you are just keeping up with your neighbors and their prayer needs, some who do not understand may perceive it as stalking. A suggestion I would make is that any sensitive information that people share with you in confidence should be keep in a confidential place.

# Understanding and Engaging Your Spiritual Spheres of Influence

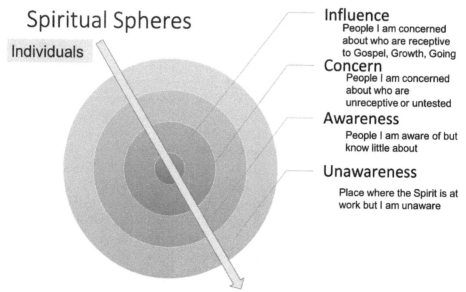

Another way to help discover a person of peace is drawing your spheres of influence. It is helpful because it anticipates and helps you to see, understand, and engage as God works to lead someone from lostness through maturity to ministry and mission. To simplify this, I would suggest that people move through four spheres of our lives. People move from a place where I am unaware of them, to a place where I am aware, to a place of concern, to a place of influence, and then out again.

Why would I even start with those of whom I am not aware? The reason is that God is aware of them and you need to be prepared for them. Remember that in Acts 3, Peter and John were completely unaware that on this day the lame man would be the catalyst for the next wave of the church. Although they were unaware, through prayer and surrender to the Holy Spirit, they were open to engage and respond to the working of God. This lame man was a person of peace who moved quickly through John and Peter's spheres of awareness and concern to their sphere of influence, as expressed in Peter words, "*Silver or gold I do not have, but what I do have I give you. In the name of Jesus Christ of Nazareth, walk.*" *(Acts 3:6 NIV).* This man's entrance into Peter's sphere of influence changed the whole schedule of that day as this lame man, himself, quickly became a source of influence. The world that knew him as the *man who used to sit begging at the temple gate called Beautiful* now saw him as a whole man, following Peter and John into the Temple, leaping with joy. Later, the presence of this former lame man stood as overwhelming proof of God's work through the Apostles and protected them from the persecution of the religious leaders (Acts 4).

While the sphere of unawareness is the place where the Spirit is at work but I am unaware, the sphere of awareness consists of people I am aware of but know little about. For me, these are the neighbors that move in and out of the apartments and rental houses around my home. I have made an effort to know them but have little information about them outside of their names. The goal of this sphere is to know more about them so that you may begin to know them. As you do, they will naturally move into your sphere of concern. This is easy for me because, as my children would say, "My dad doesn't know a stranger. They are all just friends he's never met." While I engage people to the embarrassment of my family and friends, others may struggle with initiating the first conversation.

In my sphere of concern are people who I know more intimately and personally and am concerned about. They are people I care about who are either unreceptive or untested as potential persons of peace. I know some are unreceptive because I have tried to engage them and met obstacles. This is not without benefit because now I can address the obstacles through prayer and actions if possible. The other people in my sphere of concern are people I care about but have not yet engaged to see if they are receptive persons of peace.

The people in my sphere of influence are not necessarily persons of peace, but they are the easiest to approach. These are people who will listen when I engage them. They are often family and friends who consider me a person of encouragement and guidance. Because they see me as accessible and a person they can trust, they will come to me for prayer and counsel. Some are lost while others are saved, but they have one thing in common: they see me as a person of influence and God has given me that influence in their life so that I might continually engage them as a potential person of peace.

One exercise that may help you to find people of peace is to make a list of people you know and place their names in the appropriate spheres. Starting with your sphere of *unawareness*, you pray that God makes you sensitive to the people in whom He is working. This sphere is where you trust and anticipate God's sovereign work in the lives of others but have no specific information about them. Like a soldier, you are ready every day to engage the next mission and get your marching orders from your commander. As God moves people from a place of unawareness into your sphere of *awareness*, you are prepared to know them better so that you might find inroads to help them in their spiritual development. Who are they? What are their likes and dislikes? What issues are they struggling with? What are their needs? How can I pray for them? These are a few questions you may ask in this arena of influence.

The movement from awareness to *concern* will be very natural because the more you know them and they know you, the more you will feel a sense of connection and concern. At this stage, you may be motivated to ask: What are their obstacles to belief and practice? How can I help them move to the next level of faith? In what areas do I need to challenge them? Remember your concern does not mean control. Again, this is a dance. As the Spirit leads, you follow. Seize the open doors of *influence*. Thus, at the core of influence is your opportunity to get involved in their lives. While in the other spheres you are asking questions about and of them, in this sphere they are beginning to ask questions of you: What is different about you? How can I have what you have? Can you help me?

As you list the people of your life and as you draw these spheres, you will find people already in each sphere. List the people in each sphere of your life, starting with the people of influence first and testing their receptivity. Next, pray for the people in your spheres of concern and awareness and anticipate God's movement. Finally, trust and remain surrendered to the Holy Spirit's work in your sphere of unawareness.

## CONCLUSION

Churches are dying today because they are not growing with new waves of Spirit-produced receptive people. In addition, church plants are not succeeding because they are not good at discovering and building ministries on receptive persons of peace. For the last 15 years, I have planted new churches and engaged existing ones. If one of my existing churches closed their doors today, it would be in a sea of lost people that is even larger than when they first started. Like a person dying of starvation in a field of ripe fruit, churches would die surrounded by the lost they were called to reach. In a world where Christianity is popular, the Acts model that gathers the many and develops the individual may work, but in a world that is removed from the church, the model of Jesus starting with the one, the person of peace, may be more effective. Christians need to stop inviting people to church to be disciples and start discipling the way that Jesus did. Who is your person of peace?

> *Like a person dying of starvation in a field of ripe fruit, churches would die surrounded by the lost they were called to reach.*

# SECTION 3: GETTING THE WORD INTO PEOPLE

## CHAPTER 17: CREATING A TRANSFORMATIVE COVENANT

Years ago, I attended an evangelism training course called Continuing Witnessing Training or CWT. This course was designed to train me to train witnesses. God's Plan, Our Need, and God's Provision were all topics I understood and regularly used in sharing my faith. What I realized on the day we discussed "Our Response" is that I did not know how to close the deal. While I was good at letting people know about God's loving desire for them, how sin prevented them from experiencing it, and how Jesus through His death solved this problem, I was not good at inviting them to respond. Most of my witnessing was information without invitation. Two questions that were a part of the CWT presentation changed all that and helped me to be more effective in closing the deal: "Do you understand what I have shared with you?" and "Is there any reason you would not be willing to surrender your life to Christ right now?" These questions still stand as a reminder that the reconciled, who have been given the ministry of reconciliation, have been placed on this earth not to just inform but to offer, not to just educate but to invite, and not just to share but to provide an opportunity.

> *God expects an invitation to follow the presentation of the good news.*

God expects an invitation to follow the presentation of the good news. As a matter of fact, the Gospel is not complete without offering an opportunity to respond. "For God so loved the world that He gave His one and only Son" is incomplete without "that whosoever would believe would have eternal life." It would be insane for a rescue team to get on board a sinking ship and tell its passengers about all the provisions they brought to rescue them and then depart without an invitation to use them. God expects us to share our faith and make every effort to close the deal, thus making a disciple.

While most of this discussion has been about closing the deal with a lost person, the same ideas are true concerning the growth and deployment of a disciple. Remember you could potentially encounter a person of peace in three areas: Gospel, grow, or go. As Jesus said to His disciples in John, you might be reaping where you have not sown. As Paul says in 1 Corinthians 3, you may be a planter or a waterer. The point is that we are only a part of God's plan in the life of any individual. We may move them from point A to point B while someone else may move them to points C and D. In any case, the strategy remains the same: get them into the Word in a way that gets the Word into them.

While the first previous section dealt with getting them into the Word, we will now look at getting the Word into them. Having found the person of peace, it is time to engage them and the people they will bring to the table. One of the best ways to do this is through a covenant.

### WHY A COVENANT?

To many, the idea of developing a covenant may seem extreme and unrealistic, but there are some good reasons for a written covenant.

God has always used covenants. Throughout the Old Testament, God used covenants to define His relationship with His people. He made covenants with the patriarchs and with the people He delivered from Egypt through Moses. Needless to say, while God's people often failed in their fulfillment of the covenant, God was always faithful and, even many times, gracious in spite of their failures. God's covenants throughout the Old Testament were about the spiritual growth of His people. They were about knowing Him, His purposes, and His blessing.

Covenants reflect the type of surrender that God requires of His followers. The disciples left all to follow Jesus. In light of this, wouldn't their surrender have impacted their understanding of the words of Jesus when He told them to "make disciples?" Would they have expected any less surrender or commitment from their followers than they themselves had surrendered to Christ? I have had church leaders oppose a covenant because they think it too high a commitment level for church members. I would submit to you that for many reasons, including numbers and money, we have encouraged church membership with little or no expectations at all. Salvation is free gift from God, but it does not come without expectations. Perhaps we should emphasize the name "Christian" less and emphasize more the following of Jesus and His teachings. Maybe we should expect that when someone becomes a Christian, he would regularly get into the Word in such a way that the Word gets into him so that he becomes like the Word, Jesus Christ.

> *Defining expectations through a covenant agreement can help me know when I need to stop, dust off, and move on.*

When we celebrate the Lord's Supper together, we celebrate the new covenant between God and man. In the words of Jesus, "*This is my blood of the covenant, which is poured out for many for the forgiveness of sins*" Matthew 26:28 (NIV). Although salvation has always been a product of God's grace and man's surrender and faith (*The just shall live by faith*—Romans 1:17), the new covenant spells this out in detail. The symbols that Jesus used in the Lord's Supper remind us of the formation of a new covenant between God and man based upon the sacrifice of Jesus that would provide forgiveness, allowing humanity a new relationship with God through faith.

Jesus told His disciples that if people did not receive their message, then the disciples should shake the dust off their feet—move on. Defining expectations through a covenant agreement can help me know when I need to stop, dust off, and move on. Through my years of pastoral counseling, I have learned the difference between supporting and enabling, which I can define in one word, "PROGRESS." I want to see progress. I am asking only what Jesus commanded in the Great Commission—"to teach them to obey all that I commanded." I am not talking about my commandments but God's commandments that He may use me to reveal. Observed obedience to the commands of Christ is the progress I am looking for. If I do not see it for an extended period of time, I may be in danger of enabling. Covenants can help me know where the person has stopped progressing, where I need to stop supporting, and where, if they are willing to obey and recommit, we can start again.

Covenants give me permission to speak into the lives of people. We live in a free society where we cannot force accountability; it must be something that is mutually agreed upon. Supervision and servitude can be forced from the top down, but mentoring and accountability must be volunteered from the bottom up. I can force my children to do a lot of things, like cleaning their room, but I can never force them to like it. This is the difference between obedience and honor. While in honor you will always find obedience, in obedience you will not always find honor. A covenant is an honorable agreement between two individuals that always includes an act of obedience that comes from healthy accountability and mentoring.

Throughout my book, you will hear me raising the bar when it comes to Christianity, expecting more of someone who calls himself a Christian. A covenant agreement is the most practical way to do this. It clearly defines what my responsibilities are and what I expect of a follower of Jesus. Once again, it is all about holding them accountable for getting in the Word and the Word getting in them, measured by them becoming like The WORD—Jesus Christ.

## WHAT IS A COVENANT?

What is a covenant? A covenant is a detailed yet flexible agreement that passionately guides the spiritual development of a person through mentorship and accountability. It clarifies expectations on all sides without micromanagement. It helps map and evaluate progress in our personal and ministry life.

Covenants by nature are conditional and can be expressed grammatically through conditional statements. If you do this... then I will do this....

## THE PURPOSE OF THE COVENANT

The purpose of a covenant is expressed in the previously stated mantra:

*Transformation happens when you get an individual into the Word in such a way that gets the Word into them so that they become like The Word – Jesus Christ.*

This is the reason for the covenant. Again, people who are exposed to God's Word with an open, receptive heart will produce spiritual fruit and a changed life. This changed life is measured by how much their life reflects the character of Christ.

## WHY PUT IT IN WRITING?

Dawson Trotman, the founder of The Navigators, is credited with saying, "Thoughts disentangle themselves when they pass through the lips and the fingertips." Greater clarity comes when we speak or write something. Expectations are more defined and accountability is more certain when an agreement is written.

It takes away from the "I said; you said." Document or die was a phrase I heard working for the government. Since that time, I have found that documentation can help end fights and reveal the right and wrong of situations. Google Search on my wife's cell phone has given her an unfair advantage when we argue. No longer can I just authoritatively state my opinion as fact because what used to take days and many arguments to prove me wrong now takes only a minute. Having easy access to the facts just takes all the fun out of arguing. In the same way, developing a covenant of growth takes away arguments.

A covenant gives me an opportunity to pinpoint and address reasons for failure. While pastoring in California, I developed three covenants to define expectations and help people move from salvation and membership, through growth and spiritual maturity, to influence and leadership. At each of these levels, when a person got off track, the covenant allowed me the opportunity to go to them, not in judgment but as their pastor, to help them to see where they had failed and what the next step was get them back on track.

## How to Develop a Covenant

Again, my desire is to develop an intuitive approach. Thus, I am not trying to give you something to duplicate but to reproduce with your own flavor. Examples should be seen as skeletons for you to flesh out and make your own. Because of this, the list below is there only to help you determine what works for you and the people God has placed in your life. In addition, the list below includes the full list of items and responsibilities, which may not be appropriate in the beginning stages of a transformative relationship. A simple covenant may begin the process, and as the participant grows and matures, other elements may be added.

### *Covenant Purpose*

Why are we going to meet? What do we expect from our time together? Remember, this is a discipleship or transformative covenant. Therefore, your covenant needs to include getting them into the Word and getting the Word into them. The expectation is that if these other two things are happening, the participant will demonstrate Christlikeness.

### *Participant's Name*

Who is the covenant for? Who is the Timothy in this relationship? Who is being mentored or coached?

### *Discipler's Name:*

Who is the mentor or facilitator? Who is the Paul of the relationship? Who will be leading and guiding the conversation as we meet?

### *Date of the Agreement and Length of time:*

When did we establish this covenant? How long will we meet together? What is the number of encounters and length of each? I would suggest that you keep this short, 3 to 6 weeks, and renew it as necessary. This gives a chance for you to evaluate them and them to evaluate you. I would also suggest that each meeting be no longer than an hour.

### *Time and Place Meeting*

When and where are we going to meet? This is important because it creates deadlines for all expectations to follow.

### *Reading Assignment*

The facilitator and the participant will agree upon the appropriate passages to be read for each given week. Slower readers may read a chapter a week while others may read several chapters per week. Participants are expected to read and reread the assigned passage and journal all insights and questions.

*Participant Responsibilities:*

The following should be included in this covenant
- Daily commitment to read and engage the Bible, journaling questions and insights
- Weekly meetings to share questions and insights for critique.
- Be honest, open, and surrendered to what God is saying through His Word
- Seriously consider all advice, counsel, and challenges that come from the facilitator (or group)
- To change as God empowers and enables.

*Facilitator Responsibility*

The facilitator should include the following in this covenant.
- Create a safe place and learning environment.
- Read the Bible, share, and help participants to develop knowledge and understanding of the Bible
- Listen, pray, and be a spiritual guide moving the participant inductively through the transformative process of knowledge, perspective, conviction, competence and character.
- Lead the participants to fish for themselves.
- Lead the participants into being a fishers of men.

## COVENANT EXAMPLE

---

*Covenant Purpose:* To better understand Jesus and His teachings and what they mean to me.

*Participant's Name:* John Doe       Initials: _____

*Discipler's Name:* Martin Jones     Initials: _____

*Date of the Agreement and Length of Time:* Starting January 4, 2016, for 6 weeks

*Time and Place of Meeting:* Starbucks, Arlington Rd., Akron, Ohio

*Reading Assignment:* Starting in Gospel of John, one chapter per week.

*Participant's Responsibilities:*
- Daily commitment to read and engage the Bible, journaling questions and insights
- Weekly to share questions and insights for critique
- Be honest, open, surrendered to what God is saying through His Word
- Seriously consider all advice, counsel and challenges that come from the facilitator (or group)
- To change as God empowers and enables

*Facilitator's Responsibilities:*
- Create safe place and learning environment
- Read Bible, share, and help participants to develop knowledge and understanding of the Bible
- Listen, pray, and be a spiritual guide moving the participant inductively through the Transformative Process of knowledge, perspective, conviction, competence, and character
- Lead the participant to spiritually feed themselves
- Lead the participant to engage his sphere of influence with the Good News of Jesus

# CHAPTER 18: HEALTHY CONTEXT TO BUILD TRANSFORMATIVE RELATIONSHIPS

No man is an island. It is true God created us for relationships, to love and to be loved. Just like healthy children come from healthy homes, healthy Christians develop in environments that are healthy. The environment that is conducive to transformation centers around the study of God's Word in a **safe** place where **fellowship, nurturing, accountability, and reproduction** take place.

## FELLOWSHIP

*Hebrews 10:23-25 (NIV) Let us hold unswervingly to the hope we profess, for he who promised is faithful. 24And let us consider how we may spur one another on toward love and good deeds, 25not giving up meeting together, as some are in the habit of doing, but encouraging one another—and all the more as you see the Day approaching.*

Fellowship is the getting together of individuals that produces deepening relationships. Fellowship requires time set aside out of your busy schedule. Fellowship cannot take place without appointment. How many times have you met a friend in the store and said, "Hey, let's get together" and it happened? Chances are, if you are like me, it didn't. If you assume fellowship will happen without committing time to make it happen, it probably won't. A lack of setting appointments for the people that matter has contributed to the breakup of marriages and the rebellion of teens. In 1974, Harry Chapin sung a song entitled *Cat's in the Cradle*. It was about a father who, because he has no time for his son, raises a son who has no time for his father. This song begins with an admiring son who wants be just like his father and ends with the lament of a father as he realizes that his son's wish has come true.

> *I've long since retired, my son's moved away*
> *I called him up just the other day*
> *I said I'd like to see you if you don't mind*
> *He said I'd love to dad, if I could find the time*
> *You see my new job's a hassle, and the kids have the flu*
> *But it's sure nice talking to you dad*
> *It's been sure nice talking to you*
>
> *And as I hung up the phone, it occurred to me*
> *He'd grown up just like me*
> *My boy was just like me*
>
> *And the cat's in the cradle and the silver spoon*
> *Little boy blue and the man on the moon*
> *When you coming home son, I don't know when,*
> *But we'll get together then, dad*
> *We're gonna have a good time then*

In Hebrews 10: 24-25, Paul affirms the fact that fellowship cannot happen without appointment. He saw this as a problem in the first century church and encouraged Christians to set time aside to be together. But fellowship was more than just an appointment—it was a shared experience as believers studied the teachings of Jesus and as they experienced transformation both individually and together. The Greek word for fellowship–*koinonia*–was more than just socializing together; it was learning about God and one another. In most churches today, fellowship is used to describe informal gatherings in the church, while in the New Testament it was a part of everything the group did together. In other words, New Testament fellowship was not just gathering; it was what took place when people gathered.

"We have great fellowship" is phrase I have often heard to describe churches that have been declining or are even on the brink of closure. These dying churches, even though they get together regularly, are not experiencing the Koinonia type of fellowship of the first church. While the quantity of fellowship is there in that they get together every week, the quality of fellowship, the sharing of life together, is not there. What they mean is they get along well when they get together on Sundays and special events. In contrast, the New Testament church did not just get along, they built intimate relationships with one another, shared possessions together, and even suffered together. In addition, their fellowship was contagious. People seeing the intimacy of the church wanted to be a part of it, so they also shared growth together. The context, then, for transformation must include this type of fellowship.

## SAFE PLACE

*1 John1:5-10 (NIV) This is the message we have heard from him and declare to you: God is light; in him there is no darkness at all. 6If we claim to have fellowship with him and yet walk in the darkness, we lie and do not live out the truth. 7But if we walk in the light, as he is in the light, we have fellowship with one another, and the blood of Jesus, his Son, purifies us from all sin. 8If we claim to be without sin, we deceive ourselves and the truth is not in us. 9If we confess our sins, he is faithful and just and will forgive us our sins and purify us from all unrighteousness. 10If we claim we have not sinned, we make him out to be a liar and his word is not in us.*

In order to have this kind of true, biblical fellowship, as described by the word "koinonia," a safe place must be created. What we are really talking about is confidentiality. A true biblical community is about faith in God and faith in one another. Without trust, you cannot have fellowship or nurturing. A setting must be as secure as a safe and as accepting as a mother's arms. As God's Word works on the heart of a person, revealing harmful attitudes and destructive behaviors, the environment must be one that invites sharing. It must be an environment that cultivates honesty and openness: the two key ingredients for change. We know we have achieved this environment when people admit the truth and even volunteer it.

1 John 1:5-10 tells us that like light reveals the reality of all things and like it exposes everything that is good and bad, so does God, but more than one just having a light, God in His very nature IS light that reveals. In His presence, there can be no darkness. You cannot

walk with Him without the exposure of actions and motives. The only way to walk with God is in honesty and openness. We must always be willing to tell the truth, the whole truth, and nothing but the truth. The word "confession" means, literally, to say the same thing. In this context, it means to admit what God reveals. A safe place is a place where God is free to reveal and we are free to agree with God and share with others.

# Nurturing

It is expected that when a baby is hungry that a parent will wrap a bib around his neck and feed him, but it is sad to see a bib wrapped around the neck of a grown man or woman who has experienced a head injury that precludes them from feeding themselves. While feeding a baby for the first time can be exciting for a new parent, feeding an adult who will never be able to feed themselves is sad. Healthy parenting looks forward to raising the next generation of healthy parents.

Nurturing means spiritually feeding others, teaching them to feed themselves, and then teaching them to feed others. Nurturing means caring for another in a way that produces growth, maturity, and interdependence. Nurturing moves a person from dependence through independence to interdependence. If you go to the hardware store to buy a chain, you will find several half-links under the hydraulic cutter that are leftovers from when the chain was separated during previous purchases. These half-links are dependent on the other half to be complete. While this half-link represents dependence, a whole link represents independence, and a chain would represent interdependence. While there is not much you can do with a half link, a whole link and a chain made up of several links can be helpful. Moving through these three phases is a natural part of maturing physically and spiritually.

Nurturing is a parent's appropriate response to each of these stages. A parent feeds children because they are dependent. As parents see motor skills emerging, they will give their child a spoon (better a spoon than a fork) so they can start developing skills to independently feed themselves. The process does not stop there. The goal is that they can sit around the table as a family with other independent feeders—this is interdependence. The value is that everyone in the interdependent phase is able to take care of their individual needs and enjoy the experience we call family dinner.

Nurturing spiritually is very similar to this. The nurturing leader feeds the follower with the goal of independent feeding so that one day the follower can bring to the table the skills to feed himself and enjoy the group time together. Like a parent, the leader working with the Holy Spirit feeds the new follower and watches as he develops the fine motor skills necessary to feed himself. Allow me to remind you at this point that just like teaching a child to feed themselves is messy, so also is teaching a follower to feed from God's Word. They will not always get it right, doctrine may be a little off, and application may be a bit messy, but through the leader's patient and persistent modeling and the Holy Spirit's guiding, the follower will learn to be proficient, *correctly handling the word of truth.(2 Timothy 2:15)*.

Nurturing in church that does not move a person spiritually through the process of dependence to independence to interdependence will not produce healthy Christians. Christians stuck in dependence may develop a false sense of entitlement and become spoiled consumers who see the church as only a feeding station for them and their families. Christians who get stuck in independence may become arrogant rebels without a clue, denying the advice and counsel of people God has placed in their life for support and further maturity. Their development is incomplete and stagnates. They may move from place to place attempting to turn each environment into the one that will make them happy. Both the spoiled and underdeveloped fill many of our churches because they have not been nurtured through dependence and independence to interdependence. If this is done properly, then just like healthy children grow and become healthy parents, followers grow to become healthy influencers and leaders.

## ACCOUNTABILITY

*We need people around us that when they do disagree with us, it matters so much that it drives us upward in prayer, inward to rethink our position, and outward as we look to others for a greater perspective. – Transformative Church Planting Movement*

The context of transformation must include people that are willing to push on us, our ideas, and at times our impaired thinking. I was once in a group where a seasoned veteran of recovery looked at a newbie and said, "Yes, I used to think just like that when I was an idiot, too." Then he looked the young addict in the face like a loving father and said, "I know you are sincere and really believe this to be true, but it does not make it so." That day I understood impaired thinking in a way that I had not before. I understood that addicts are good at being sincerely WRONG. I needed the confrontation that man offered even though it was not directed at me. It caused me to open my heart and rethink the things that I believed about God, me, and others. It was encounters like this that humbled me and helped turn my stony heart to one of clay that God could now remold.

This is accountability and must be present in any setting where God's Word is being engaged. As sinners, we have developed attitudes and thinking that support our wrong deeds. God uses the sharpness of the Word (Hebrews 4:12), the conviction of the Spirit (John 16:8), and the accountability of others (Eph. 4:15) to break up the hardness of impaired thinking so that, as Paul says in Romans 12, we may stop conforming, start transforming, think new thoughts, and know God's will.

*Romans 12: 2-3 (NIV) Do not conform to the pattern of this world, but be transformed by the renewing of your mind. Then you will be able to test and approve what God's will is—his good, pleasing and perfect will.*

## REPRODUCTION

Fellowship is important, but it can have a downside. When a group of people care for one another, it can create a gravitational pull that can turn that community into a clique. By nature, humans avoid pain and move toward pleasure, so they steer clear of crises and camp in comfort. We want to stay where we are comfortable and avoid the uncomfortable, and hanging out with the same crowd or clique is comfortable. It is for this reason that at times relationships and fellowship can work against outreach and evangelism. It is often more comfortable to hang out with Christians than it is to engage non-Christians. The church of

Acts suffered this phenomenon and became complacent. While Jesus said the disciples would be His witnesses not just in Jerusalem and Judea but also Samaria, even to the ends of earth, the disciples seemed to be satisfied with the ministry of the first church of Jerusalem. Is it any wonder that God allowed persecution to scatter the church when they got too comfortable with who they were already with?

God intended for the church be like a family. I want my home to be a safe, nurturing place where my children can fellowship with me and their siblings. I also want it to be a place where there is accountability and encouragement to do right things. Ultimately, I want it to be a healthy launching pad from which my children take off to build their own healthy families and homes. My success is not complete until my healthy children are raising healthy children.

I would submit to you that a healthy group of Christians will never continually look the same. Like all living things, they will grow and change. Fellowship done right will attract and relationships done right will expand. Any group of Christians that remains the same over a long period of time is unhealthy. Reproduction is as natural to the church as fellowship and relationships are. Healthy things gather, grow, and go. In Jesus' parable of the talents, the Master criticized the one servant who did not risk but instead buried the Master's talent. His lack of faith led him preserve the master's talent in order to keep everything the same (Matthew 25:14-30). Talents could be the people that God gives our group who need to move on for the purpose of reproduction. Stop preserving and start investing!

Transformation happens in this type of family environment where people experience a safe place, where deep friendships are developed through consistent fellowship, where they are held accountable for the truth God reveals, and where they reproduce, wanting others to experience the same.

## CHAPTER 19: TRANSFORMATIVE BIBLICAL MODEL

On July 4, 1776, the Declaration of Independence was signed by a bunch of traitors and seditionists to the Crown of England. In signing this document, the men we call Fathers and Patriots were risking all. Their signature meant their death if they lost the war, and the war would have been lost if the message of freedom contained in this document did not get into the hearts of the early American farmers and store owners, transforming them into soldiers. In essence, the American Revolution was a grassroots movement of freedom.

Christians also have a message of freedom that started a revolution. 2000 years ago, the architect of our Declaration of Independence, as part of the plan to secure our opportunity for freedom, died on the cross. He did not just sign a document risking His death; He died guaranteeing freedom for His followers and revolutionaries. Our Declaration of Independence is the Bible, with its core message being the Gospel or Good News. With this message, we have the power to defeat the greatest foe of freedom everywhere. We can defeat the being behind every evil tyrant and evil action. Through the death of Jesus, we can defeat sin, self, and Satan. Just like in the American Revolution, however, we must do more than get people into the message; we must get the message into them.

The parable of the sower is all about getting the message of God's Word into the hearts of man in a way that transforms life. Again, let me remind you that this message of freedom is not just about freedom from the penalty of sin, nor just about the future freedom from the presence of sin; it is also about daily freedom from the power of sin. The parable is about getting the Word into a person producing regeneration, glorification, and sanctification. Below is Jesus' commentary on this parable. Using it and the parallel passages in Luke and Mark, we see Him defining the characters of and obstacles to transformation.

*Matthew 13:18-23 (NIV) 18 "Listen then to what the parable of the sower means: 19When anyone hears the message about the kingdom and does not understand it, the evil one comes and snatches away what was sown in his heart. This is the seed sown along the path. 20The one who received the seed that fell on rocky places is the man who hears the word and at once receives it with joy. 21But since he has no root, he lasts only a short time. When trouble or persecution comes because of the word, he quickly falls away. 22The one who received the seed that fell among the thorns is the man who hears the word, but the worries of this life and the deceitfulness of wealth choke it, making it unfruitful. 23But the one who received the seed that fell on good soil is the man who hears the word and understands it. He produces a crop, yielding a hundred, sixty, or thirty times what was sown."*

Jesus defines the characters of this story. In the book of Luke, Jesus defines the seed as the *Word of God* (Luke 8:11) making the farmer, planter, or sower God Himself. Then He defines the soil as the heart of man. It is an amazing and humbling thought to think that the God of the universe would invest His Word into our lives. As a farmer invests his time and seed into a soil and expects it to be transformed and to produce, God expects that His Word, planted in a well-cultivated heart, will produce something abundant and transformed. The difference between a seed and a plant is transformation. God expects His Word, in the  heart of man, to transform and produce fruit and more seeds in abundance. I would be remiss if I did not point out that this is a natural and normal process. Just like it is natural for a seed to change and become a plant, it is natural and normal for God's Word to transform and produce.

The parable is all about getting the Word into a person's life in such a way that produces. The problem is that sin has affected the soil condition, and the soil is full of obstacles that prevent the healthy development of God's Word. Jesus describes these obstacles as hardness that prevents penetration, rocks below the surface that prevent root development, and weeds that prevent fruit.

Enter the discipler, the laborer in the field of God. It is our job to work with the Holy Spirit to eliminate obstacles that stop the natural course of the Word to transform and produce. As I wrote in my previous book:

*It is the role of the discipler to addresses these issues by getting dirty in the hearts of humanity. Making a disciple requires exposing a person to the Word of God and then working with the Holy Spirit getting our hands dirty cultivating, digging rocks, and pulling weeds. We must be prepared to address the hardness that comes from ignorance, misconceptions, vain rituals and traditions. We must be willing to go deeper, addressing the issues illuminated by the Spirit of God through the Word of God. We must be willing to confront wrong priorities and misplaced values that distract people from bearing the fruit of the transformed life.* – Transformative Church Planting Movement

Farming is messy work. If you are going to do it, you had better be prepared to get dirty. As Christians, we are called to work with God, the farmer, who is speaking to transform, not just inform. Thus, working with the Holy Spirit, we are called to get dirty in the messy lives of others.

## CHAPTER 20: HARDNESS OF THE HEART

I was never a farmer, but I was raised by one, and while you can take the farmer off the farm, you cannot take the farm out of the farmer. At least this was true of my father. While we did not live on a farm, we farmed every part of the small property our house did not sit on. While our neighbors grew grass, we grew corn, peas, butterbeans, okra, peaches, watermelon, grapes, potatoes, and more. I do not know what it is like to be a farmer plowing his field, but I do know what it was like getting behind a 7 1/2 HP rototiller trying to break up hard West Texas ground. Every year this same dry, hard ground had to be broken up and replanted.

Hardness is not just a problem for farmers; it has often been a problem for pastors and teachers who every week preach and teach the Word of God hoping that some of it will get in, take root, and bear fruit. As ministers, we are often the rototiller that God uses to break up the hard-hearted so that the Word can get in. So, what causes hardness in the heart, and what can we do to cultivate this soil?

## WHAT CAUSES HARDNESS?

### *Idolatry*

One thing that hardness, rocks, and weeds have in common, besides that they are all obstacles to producing fruit, is that they all reflect something other than God's Word to rely on. At its core, this is idolatry. There is actually a spectrum produced here. Hardness is the idolatry that rejects the truth of God completely for another truth, while rocks below the surface is idolatry that conditionally accepts the truth of God until it attacks our truth. Weed-filled ground accepts the truth but gives this truth no more authority than any other truth in a person's life. In contrast, good soil totally embraces God's truth as the primary catalyst for change.

What makes hardness in the heart of man? In general, hardness comes from some form of idolatry, i.e., faith and confidence in things other than God. In the Old Testament, idolatry among the children of Israel was never the complete abandonment of Yahweh God but a blending of ideologies known as syncretism. Syncretism is the merger, or blending, of different religions, cultures, or schools of thought, creating something new. The God that humiliated Egypt, delivered the children of Israel, and led them in the conquest and possession of the land became their God of war while Baal became the god of everyday life. In their eyes, Baal provided the rain for crops while Yahweh protected them from their enemies. This is one reason that in times of peace the Israelites ignored God—they did not need His immediate protection.

> *While we would condemn the pagan who is worshiping an idol in rejection of the true God, we worship a god we create with partial acceptance of the True God.*

Throughout history, syncretism has been the preferred form of idolatry for those that call themselves followers of God and Christians. While we would condemn the pagan who is worshiping an idol in rejection of the true God, we worship a god we create with partial acceptance of the True God. We worship an amalgamation of Christianity and our culture and traditions. Hardness, then, comes from OUR solidified idea of God. Hardness comes from the fact that our god is our creation in our image, and we are comfortable with the mix. It is our recipe of god passed on from generation to generation, changing only as it fits our lifestyle. We prefer the god of our own creation, the one we make up, rather than the one that really is.

The Pharisees worshiped the system they created more than the God of the Old Testament. Symbols became sacraments, and feasts and festivals God designed for remembrance became avenues of entitlement, as in, "God, I did what you told me to do, so you owe me." After the hard work that came from traveling and participating in the festivals and feasts, the children of Israel felt they had earned the right to eternal life. The Pharisees were so focused on the traditions of God, they lost sight of the God of the traditions.

How did Jesus address the hardness produced by this type of idolatry? Just like concrete must be broken before it can be removed and ground must be broken before a seed can be planted, the heart of an individual must be broken before it becomes receptive to the truth. Just like hardness can be broken only by that which is harder, Jesus met the hardness of these religious leaders and the idolatry it created with hardness in return. He confronted them with the hard truth about themselves and their religion.

Jesus did not confront the Pharisees to win debates and show His intellectual superiority but to show He loved them. Although I would agree that Jesus confronted in order to contrast their false theology and practices with God's truth, He ultimately did it as an expression of His love for them. Jesus loved these religious leaders enough to oppose them. While Jesus tells us to *love those who despitefully use and persecute* us, it does not mean never challenging them. While you and I want to avoid false teachers, Jesus engaged them. Although He never gave in to their anger, He was always ready and willing to confront their false teachings and bad practices.

*Solidification Produced by Comfort*

I like to be comfortable. The things that make me comfortable are like magnets drawing me toward them; once there, they encourage me to stay. Comfort is a warm bed on a cold winter morning when I stay under the covers and make Karen get up first to make coffee. Moreover, the older I get, the more I am willing to exchange vehicle efficiency and gas mileage for comfort. Yes, I like comfort.

The problem is that comfort can stop movement and cause solidification, and you cannot be immovable and hard and be a follower of Jesus. Many people are hard and unreceptive because they are comfortable, but being a follower of Jesus and His teaching means transformation. You cannot have transformation without change, and you cannot change without being willing to become uncomfortable. Hardness may be a product of a comfortable life where people do not want you to rock their boat with the challenge of change. It is not beyond God to allow uncomfortable situations to come into our lives to break up solidification produced by comfort.

## BREAKING UP HARDNESS

*Test Hardness*

Terry Travis lived across the street from me while I was planting a church in Texas. He was a big guy, and all my initial encounters with him seemed to communicate that he would be a tough nut to crack. One day I went over to a garage sale at his home where he and his brother were sitting behind a table waiting for customers. It was the most intimidating shopping experience I've ever had. I was afraid to buy something because I would have to face these two burly men. I was afraid not to buy something for the same reason. I think I picked up something I did not need, rounded up so I would not have to worry about getting change, paid quickly, and went home. Later on, our church planned a "Bring a Neighbor Day" as an outreach. I knew that I had to model this and really needed to invite someone. That week as I prayed concerning who to invite, God impressed on my heart, "Invite Terry." So, like a good church planter, I prayed for clarity, and once again God said, "Invite Terry." Knowing this, I started looking for opportunities to invite him.

One day I looked out my front window, once again hoping no one was home so I could tell God I tried, but there was Terry in his front yard. I knew this would be the day. I then mustered up as much testosterone as I could, which was probably adrenaline, took up my cross, and walked across the street expectantly (to fail). Armed with the attitude of "Let's get this over with," I approached Terry, and when he acknowledged my presence, I said with a quivering voice, "Terry, tomorrow (because I waited till the last minute) my church is having a Bring a Friend Day, and I would like for you and your family to come and be my friends." My well-planned delivery was perfect. While I was not expecting much, Terry looked down at me and said, "My wife and I have been talking about going to church. We would love to come. What time?" Shocked but encouraged, I decided to push my luck and said, "Well, Terry, Sunday School starts at 9:45, and I would love for you guys to come to that, but if not, the service is at 11:00." He replied, "We will see you at 9:45." Over the next several months,

I baptized Terry, his wife, and children, and he eventually became a key leader in my church, teaching young adults in Sunday School.

What I thought was a hard nut turned out to be a marshmallow, fruit so ripe for the picking that when I just touched it, it fell off. This experience taught me the lesson that God taught Samuel about His calling of David: "Man looks on the outside but God looks on the heart" (1 Sam. 16:7 NIV). I realized that what appears to be hardness needs to be tested. What might appear to be hard to us may just be a crusty top layer that once broken through reveals the activity of the Holy Spirit and His drawing of a person to faith in Christ.

## Hit It Head On: Healthy Debate/Confrontation of Ideology

*John 9:1-6 (NIV) As he went along, he saw a man blind from birth. 2 His disciples asked him, "Rabbi, who sinned, this man or his parents, that he was born blind?" 3 "Neither this man nor his parents sinned," said Jesus, "but this happened so that the works of God might be displayed in him. 4 As long as it is day, we must do the works of him who sent me. Night is coming, when no one can work. 5 While I am in the world, I am the light of the world." After saying this, he spit on the ground, made some mud with the saliva, and put it on the man's eyes. 7 "Go," he told him, "wash in the Pool of Siloam" (this word means "Sent"). So the man went and washed, and came home seeing.*

Didn't Jesus know that making mud on the Sabbath was breaking the oral law of the Pharisees? Was He unaware it was illegal for a man to carry his bed on the Sabbath or rub one's hands over a stalk of grain or an ear of corn to get a meal? Of course, He knew, but He did it anyway. Although Jesus never violated the Old Testament law, He wreaked havoc on the religious traditions developed around the law. Doesn't sound very missional to me. As a matter of fact, it sounds like Jesus was trying to pick a fight. It does, probably because He was. We know these actions often ended in a verbal debate and sometimes devolved into an attempt to physically hurt or kill Jesus. What we must remember is that these actions that challenged the religious people of Jesus' day were accompanied by even greater acts revealing God's glory in Jesus. He healed a lame man and then told the man to take up his bed and walk. In John 9, Jesus kneaded mud, placed it on the eyes of a blind man, and then told the man to go and wash. After washing, this 40-year-old man, who had been blind from birth, saw for the first time. In all these cases, the overwhelming miracles, the signs that God was walked among them, were rejected over the technicalities. Again, when it comes to the story of the blind man, the Pharisees continued to ask him, "How did He heal you?" to which he responded, "He made mud." Thus, kneading this small amount of mud on the Sabbath was their whole rationale for rejecting Christ. Healthy confrontation like this picked away at the hardness produced by religious tradition. It may have been these encounters that led Nicodemus and other religious leaders like the ones mentioned in Acts 6 to become believers in Christ.

> *...sounds like Jesus is trying to pick a fight*

Likewise, we must be ready to confront people's solidified ideology with the truth of Christ. I have a friend who believes in God but not in Jesus. Oh, he does not have a problem with Jesus and His teachings—he just does not believe that Jesus is God. I know where he stands and he knows where I stand. I am often confronting him with the claims of Christ and the impact that God has had on my life through Jesus the divine. I pray that one day my friend will soften in this area and the divine, loving Jesus will penetrate the hardness of his stance.

## *Warn of Judgment/Inform of Consequences*

A life without surrender to Christ produces an eternity without Him. At times, hardness needs to be broken up with reality, and one reality is that life is short and judgment is coming. Sometimes the good life needs to be broken up by the knowledge of accountability to come. Sometimes God may call us to inform others of coming consequences in hope of creating the nagging pain that eventually brings change. When Jesus sent the 70, He did not just tell them to shake the dust from their feet. He also added that judgment was coming. This message may be the hammer needed to break up the hardness of a soul. Some may criticize the hellfire and brimstone message, but, at times, it is the thing that is needed to break up hardness.

## *Find the Cracks: Seize Opportunities*

Years ago I bought a wood-burning stove and began to gather wood for the winter. It was at this time that I learned all the ways that wood can warm you apart from just burning it. It warms you when you cut down the tree, when you cut it up into logs, when you split the logs into firewood, and when you stack the firewood. I thought I was man enough to split my logs by hand like the pioneers did, but I quickly realized I was no frontiersman and rented a log splitter from Home Depot. In the process of my learning, I did find out that if you can find the crack in a log and drive a wedge in it, it will split much easier.

Not only is this true of logs, it is also true for splitting the hardness of a heart. Finding the cracks will help break up hardness. By cracks, I am really referring to the inadequacies of a life apart from God. We will never be all that God created us to be without His presence on the throne of our lives. Similarly, anything we place on that throne, including ourselves, will eventually fail us, proving it to be an inadequate substitute for the real God. This inadequacy of a false god is the place to put the wedge in to split the hardness of a heart. The failure of idols to quench the thirst of a soul or to satisfy the hunger of a heart is the crack to look for. When we find it, we must seize the opportunity to point them in the direction of the Bread of Life and the Living Water.

Sometimes you can **seize the opportunity produced by abundance.** Years ago I heard a pastor in an affluent area of Southern California say, "When guests come to my church, it is because their 2nd home in the mountains or their beach house could not satisfy their need for peace and rest." Sometimes God gives people all they want so they can realize it is not all they need. In a society that assumed wealth and prosperity meant divine blessings, a rich, young religious man came to Jesus to ask, "What must I do to be saved?" (Mt. 19:16). Obviously, what he had was not enough. Dissatisfaction, a feeling of purposeless, discontentment, and unhappiness break up hardness and create opportunities for God's Word to penetrate.

Sometimes you can **seize the opportunity produced by pain.** One day, while repairing a broken spring on my old, extremely heavy garage door, I raised the door, climbed the ladder, and released the whole spring assembly. I immediately noticed that I had forgotten to brace the door, and with only one set of springs to hold it, it begin to move downward, pulling me sideways off the ladder. Thinking fast, I let go, which increased the speed of the door, and it slammed shut. Being somewhat in shock, embarrassed by my stupidity, and afraid that I had destroyed the door to my garage, I ran to the outside and deadlifted the door with only one set of springs helping me. Then I realized that I still had not gotten boards to hold it open, so I slowly let it back down until the weight was too much and it slammed shut again. So, I got a board, did the deadlift thing again, and braced for my repairs. After doing this twice, I noticed pain in my lower back. This back pain was different from previous pain, not severe, but chronic; it began to affect everything I did. It was my constant companion whether I was sitting, standing, or sleeping; it was a nagging reminder that something was seriously wrong. This persistent, plaguing pain opened my mind to something I had sworn I would never consider—surgery. Sometimes pain is the only thing that will open our heart to the fact that something is wrong and things need to change.

> *...pain can be a blessing in a fallen world.*

You see, people do not change when they see the light of truth. They change when they feel the heat of the consequences of truth. I have never met a person who, after slamming a finger in a car door, said, "Boy, let's do that again." Most of us, with the exception of a weird few, move away from pain and toward pleasure. The key word is "move." Pain will make us move when nothing else can. Pain is the great incentive for change.

Pain is a result of evil in our world, but in and of itself, pain is not evil. It can be a good thing; pain can be a blessing in a fallen world. Like the warning light in the car that my wife ignores, it is not the problem—it just tells you one exists. Furthermore, physical pain is a major diagnostic tool used by doctors to tell you what and where the problem is. In fact, people who do not feel pain at all are not considered healthy. Pain gets our attention and breaks up hardness as nothing else can.

When hurting people come our way, we do not need to throw platitudes their way like, "Oh, it will be alright." Well, maybe if they do not change, it won't. Instead, we should be looking for the source of their pain. It may be personal sin. As a pastor, I have had people in my office weeping and through their tears ask me, "Why has God done this to me?" Knowing their story, I have often replied, "Well, He didn't. You did it to yourself." Then speaking the truth in love, I would attempt to help them retrace their steps from effect back to the cause. Once there, we have an opportunity to deal with the real problem of sin, and through forgiveness and surrender to God and His Word, we can begin the work of transformation.

## *Let Them Go for Another Time*

There are times in our ministry when God calls us to let people go so that they might experience consequences in hopes they will change. There are times in the Old Testament when God says He will let His children go to the idols they have created to see if the idols can help them. In Romans 1, Paul then points out how man has ignored God's obvious presence, attributing creation to the creature. His great wrath is displayed in letting them go and leaving man to his own demise. I think it is amazing that God is so great that His absence is judgment. What happens when God, the Creator and Sustainer of all things, stops sustaining? Sometimes God judges to show the world His power and glory, and sometimes He judges to get the attention of man, who is worshiping gods of his own creation.

If God Himself, who could change our attitudes and actions, chooses not to, then who are you and I to think we can? There are times when all the words, love, and concern that you can pour into a person's life will not change their mind. All the internal worry and outward nagging only hurts you and wastes energy and resources that could be reserved for when the person we love decides to make a change. Learning to let go and acknowledge limitations is an expression of faith in God. Letting go does not mean doing nothing; it means changing our strategy from actions to prayer.

The attitude of a common prayer used in AA's is about constructively letting go of people and things.

*Serenity Prayer by Reinhold Niebuhr (1892-1971)*

*God grant me the serenity to accept the things I cannot change; courage to change the things I can; and wisdom to know the difference. Living one day at a time; enjoying one moment at a time; accepting hardships as the pathway to peace; taking, as He did, this sinful world as it is, not as I would have it; trusting that He will make all things right if I surrender to His Will; that I may be reasonably happy in this life and supremely happy with Him forever in the next. Amen.*

Letting go requires the wisdom of God, His Word, and His Spirit. The information in this section is not a checklist of things to try to break up hardness but rather an attempt to build greater awareness so that we might join God in His work in the lives of those around us.

## CHAPTER 21: REMOVING ROCKS: ADDRESSING SHALLOWNESS

*The rocky soil is the hidden hardness, issues below the surface that are stopping penetration preventing the development of roots. While hardness and weeds may be easy to spot, shallowness produced by rocks is more difficult and may require testing. – Transformative Church Planting Movement*

From the moment I saw John at my church, I was as excited to have him there as he was to be there. I needed help, and he seemed primed and ready. Anything I asked him to do, he did with joy and enthusiasm. He liked hanging out with me, and I enjoyed him as a parishioner and friend. This went on for a while, and then, all the sudden, John fell off the radar. I called him and found that what used to be engaging conversations about God and the Word became filled with frustration and sadness. After a few weeks of working with John, he was back to the John I knew and enjoyed. Then, without warning, he was gone again. I called and engaged, and with joy he returned; all was good for a while and…

I do not remember if this cycled 2 or 3 times (I am a slow learner) before I chose to do something different with John that I have used with other individuals since with a great deal of success. Because insanity is doing the same thing over and over expecting different results, I decided to kick it up a notch and risk a friendship in order to get to the truth. So I sat down with John and started by sharing a time in my life when a consistent, addictive habit was destroying my character. I talked about a time when I was longing to soar with God, but every time I got off the ground, the weight of my habit pulled me back to earth. I shared with him that my life was punctuated with extremes of excitement and involvement and despair and abandonment. I then looked him in the eyes and asked, "Is there a consistent habit or hang-up that is holding you down?" I even added, "I am not asking you to tell me what it is. I am just asking you if it exists." Since John, I have used this many times, and, just like John did on this occasion, once someone admits it exists, they have no problem telling me about the problem, habit, hang-up and sin that is so easily besetting them.

John, like most of these individuals, wanted to change. He wanted to follow Jesus. In fact, this is one reason Jesus said, "[W]ith joy they receive the Word." They want the truth of God, but they are powerless to implement it.

John was an example of a person who struggled with rocks under the surface. What do rocks look like? The rocky soil is the hidden hardness or issues below the surface that are preventing the development of roots. This person is excited to hear the truth and will engage it and allow it to engage him only until it becomes uncomfortable. As the truth approaches the real issues that need to be exposed and surrendered, he stops the process.

> *Like water pressure through pipes will expose weak spots producing leaks, God allows persecution to expose our lack of faith and surrender.*

These issues are often habits, hang-ups, and problems that have plagued the individual for years. These rocks have never been removed; they are hardness that has solidified and been pushed below the surface. Unlike the hard soil, these rocks or issues cannot be cultivated—they must be removed. The person may not even be aware of the seriousness of these issues and the habits they produce because of years of denial.

The pressure created by affliction and persecution is the test for this condition. Like water pressure through pipes will expose weak spots producing leaks, God allows persecution to expose our lack of faith and surrender. Peter was a good example of this. The problem with Peter was conditional surrender; as long as Jesus was heading in the direction of the ruling Messiah, Peter was on board. Armed with the attitude that he knew more about Jesus' purpose on earth than Jesus Himself, he would often confront and rebuke Jesus when Jesus spoke of suffering and dying. When Jesus refused to stand up for Himself in the garden and rebuked Peter for doing so, Peter's faith began to waver, and this one who used to be a part of the inner circle of Jesus now followed from a distance. While Peter was waiting outside the court, John went to get him so he could be closer to the master during His trial. It was in this context that Peter's love for and devotion to Jesus was tested. It was the pressure of persecution, as three individuals accused him of being an associate of Jesus, that revealed his conditional surrender and limited devotion to Jesus. This man, who on a number of occasions confessed a willingness to die for Jesus and His cause, discovered through persecution the shallowness of his own roots as he was broken by his denial. Like the roots of a tree are tested by the wind, the depth of our faith in God's truth is always revealed by the winds of trouble and persecution. For some, persecution affirms their faith, showing them to be rooted followers of Jesus, such as the Apostles in Acts 4 who rejoiced that they were worthy to suffer like Jesus. For others it is the test that reveals their faithlessness and unwillingness to surrender all to God. Persecution and tribulation may be like tweezers going after a splinter; the closer you get to it, the more painful it is. This pain may cause many to withdraw and thus not deal with it, which then may fester and infect the whole body.

## COUNSEL WITH THE WORD

How do you deal with these rocks below the surface? Just like removing the rocks in a field may require several people and tools, the removing of issues preventing God's truth from penetrating also requires people and tools. The tool is the Word of God; the people are the Holy Spirit and Spirit-filled believers.

As a teenager and young man, I developed some bad habits that I never dealt with, even when I rededicated my life to Christ and surrendered to the ministry. Because I was being trained to be a minister, these rocks got covered with layer upon layer of denial, preventing God's Word from really transforming me. The result was that I knew a lot about God but did not really know Him and His power. Every time I would experience the truth of His Word, I received it with gladness but found it to be powerless as it hit against the solidified habits just below the surface. The hypocrisy of knowing and even teaching it without living it was depressing, and it would have destroyed my ministry, my marriage, and me if it were not for an event that drove me to a Christian counselor and a group of men who struggled with the same issues.

Although there was not a direct encounter with God's Word each session, it was biblically-based counseling that drove me to look at the Word of God and its truth about me and my problems. God used this counselor and this group of men to push me deeper into the Bible to confront me with the truth that convicted my heart and revealed changes I needed to make to my behavior. Through the Word, the Holy Spirit, a counselor, and a group, God removed the layers of dirt, exposed the rocks, and empowered me to make changes to deal with them. I found that through the same process, I could deal with many issues that prevented God's Word from taking root and bearing fruit.

The Bible speaks to most, if not all, issues of life. Once you have discovered the rocks preventing roots, use the Word to address them. Anger, bitterness, and obsessive, addictive behaviors can all be rocks under the surface. Have a person read and reread scriptures dealing with these issues and dialog about them. Use the transformative process in the next section to inductively move them from knowledge to perspective to conviction to competence. Allow God's Word and God's Spirit to convict and show them what steps they need to take or what they need to do or stop doing. As you teach them to deal with one rock effectively, they will learn how to deal with more.

# CHAPTER 22: DIGGING WEEDS: ADDRESSING DISTRACTIONS

*Matthew 13: 22 (NIV) The one who received the seed that fell among the thorns is the man who hears the word, but the worries of this life and the deceitfulness of wealth choke it, making it unfruitful.*

*Luke 8:14 (NIV) The seed that fell among thorns stands for those who hear, but as they go on their way they are choked by life's worries, riches and pleasures, and they do not mature.*

What do weeds look like? Weeds are the things that compete with the real plant. While hardness and rocks prevent roots, weeds prevent fruit. After all this work—the cultivating, planting, and watering—and after the sprout forms and the plant begins to mature, this weedy soil halts the process and nullifies all this work and God's investment (the seed) by allowing weeds to rob the plant of what it needs to bear fruit. This soil represents the heart of distraction that refuses to make God's Word and work a priority. Weeds are the idols that compete for the attention and affections of a person. In Matthew and Luke, we see that Jesus identifies some major distractions of life that prevent God's Word and work. Furthermore, what is important to note is that many distractions are not evil, just good things in the wrong place.

> **Good things in the wrong place are wrong and can produce an ineffective and unfruitful life.**

## THE DISTRACTION OF THE GOOD

Weeds represent the idolatry that is a product of bad priorities and is often the choosing of the good over the best. The greatest enemy of the best is often the good, not the bad. Good things in the wrong place are wrong and can produce an ineffective and unfruitful life.

We all seek good things in life. In fact, our country was founded upon the premise that we have the right to pursue good things. From the Declaration of Independence, we read:

*We hold these truths to be self-evident, that all men are created equal, that they are endowed by their Creator with certain unalienable Rights, that among these are Life, Liberty and the pursuit of Happiness.*

The only way to really assure the rights bestowed to us by the Creator is through the Creator. It is only in God through Christ that we can have real life, true liberty, and genuine happiness. Until He and His Word have first place in our lives, then our life, liberty and pursuit of happiness is in vain. The challenge is in letting go of or reprioritizing the good things in order to get the best. Transformation can take place only when a person is willing to let go of all that they think is essential to life in order to surrender to the Creator of real life. We must realize that real life comes from surrendering life itself, i.e., all that you are and all that you have, to the benevolent God who will in turn give it back to you with real meaning and purpose.

Allow me to lay a theological foundation for this using the importance of family. A good relationship with my wife and children is of utmost importance, but, as an end in itself, it is lacking. Like the first Adam, God created you to experience Him first, then others second (Eve). He never intended Adam to be alone; He just wanted Adam to know Him first. God did not create Eve in the same way He did Adam; He created Eve out of Adam's body. Why did He do it His way? God could have created Eve the way He created Adam or the other animals, but instead He used Adam's rib as the raw materials for her creation. Doing it this way allowed Adam, the creation of God, to take part in the creation of Eve. In doing this, Adam could now understand God and His love for His Creation, including himself, in a whole new light. Creating Eve as God did was not only so Adam would not be alone, it was also so he could know what it felt like for God to love and care for His creation. *This is now bone of my bones and flesh of my flesh; she shall be called 'woman,' for she was taken out of man* (Genesis 2:23 NIV). This is not just a statement of declaration—it is a statement of identification with the creative process of God. This is not so farfetched as some may think. The fact is that God, who created all, uses all He creates to teach all He has created. He has given us good things like husbands, wives, and children to teach us about the relationship He desires with us. These intimate relationships on earth reflect our relationship with God and help us to understand how He feels about us.

At this point, let me remind you of the difference between desire and need. God does not need us, but He does desire us, while man, who often does not desire God, desperately needs Him. When a husband and wife conceive and give birth to a child, they, on some level, can identify with the Creator of all things. Although they did not create this child *ex nihilo*, or out of nothing, they did by the design of God combine the raw materials that were needed to create a person. Not only can they identify with the Creator in His work of creation, they can also identify with God in His affection for that creation. What healthy parent would not give of his life or give up all his life for his child? I never fully understood the sacrifices that my parents made for me until I made sacrifices for my children. I never understood what my parents put up with in me until I, as a parent, had to put up with my own children. What amazes me even more is that all these things are but shadows and reflections of the great sacrifices that God has made for me and the great tolerance He has shown to me.

Family is a reflection, not the origin. Like the full moon that gives sufficient light in the night but cannot compare to the light of day, God created the family as a reflection of our relationship with Him. While these reflections are a wonderful, tangible means to greater understanding of God, they are inadequate as an end in themselves. When the good reflections of this life become the focus of life, truly the good becomes the enemy of the best. On the other hand, if I understand and appreciate the reflection, it can help me understand and enjoy reality. Family can be a great tool for understanding God. Having parents who love me and being a loving parent, I have been given two opportunities to understand the unconditional love of God. The good things of this life can be the greatest distractions or they can be the best teaching tools for our present life with Christ and the eternal life to come.

## ANXIETY/WORRY

Years ago, I learned that worry was my attempt to play God and that I do not have the resources for the job. Think about it. Worrying is our attempt to change things by thinking about them. Who among us would not like our mutant ability to be telekinesis—the ability to move things with our mind? But the truth is we do not have this ability, and it only frustrates us when we try to change things that are completely out of our control. It is a waste. Worry just takes and gives back nothing. It wears you out before your workday begins.

Imagine with me a sphere within a sphere. In the inner sphere are the things that I can control while in the outer sphere are things that I cannot control. Every day, people and situations are passing through both spheres. Allow me to illustrate this point. While we all have people we are concerned about such as a child, a brother, a sister, or a mother and father, we can exercise control or influence only as they enter our inner sphere of control. When they come to your home or office and sit down wanting advice and counsel, they are in your sphere of control. When they get up and leave, they exit your sphere of control and enter the sphere that is out of your control. Yes, while you are still concerned, you can do nothing about it except wait until they re-enter your sphere of control.

There are two things we do to move things into our sphere of control: worry and nag. We think that if we think about it long enough and hard enough by worrying, we can move what we are concerned about into our sphere of control. We obsess over every scenario and fixate over all the facts. We try to create opportunities with our mind, but to no avail, because we have forgotten that only God can think something into being. It just emotionally wears us down.

*Matthew 6: 25-34 (NIV) "Therefore I tell you, do not worry about your life, what you will eat or drink; or about your body, what you will wear. Is not life more than food and the body more than clothes? 26 Look at the birds of the air; they do not sow or reap or store away in barns, and yet your heavenly Father feeds them. Are you not much more valuable than they? 27 Can any one of you by worrying add a single hour to your life? 28 "And why do you worry about clothes? See how the flowers of the field grow. They do not labor or spin. 29 Yet I tell you that not even Solomon in all his splendor was dressed like one of these. 30 If that is how God clothes the grass of the field, which is here today and tomorrow is thrown into the fire, will he not much more clothe you—you of little faith? 31 So do not worry, saying, 'What shall we eat?' or 'What shall we drink?' or 'What shall we wear?' 32 For the pagans run after all these things, and your heavenly Father knows that you need them. 33 But seek first his kingdom and his righteousness, and all these things will be given to you as well. 34 Therefore do not worry about tomorrow, for tomorrow will worry about itself. Each day has enough trouble of its own.*

There is something else we do in an attempt to move something into our sphere of control—we NAG. Nagging is worry turned outward with words. We will obsess and complain in our attempt to bring about change. At times, this may appear to bring success, but, in truth, it does not wear just us out; it wears others out, too. Through worry, we bow at the idol of self and pray to self. If this does not get the desired result, we make our idolatrous prayers public through nagging.

# DECEITFULNESS OF RICHES

Being distracted by the deceitfulness of riches does not mean that a person is greedy; the emphasis is that he is deceived by money. This is a common problem today. Who does not worry about money? Who does not think that a little more would make them feel better or make them more secure? We think, "With more money I could relax." Jesus recognized this deception in His day and spent a considerable amount of time addressing it throughout His ministry.

In Luke 12:13-21, Jesus uses a parable that describes the deception of wealth. In it, He tells the story of a farmer who had a bumper crop one year. It was so big that he began to plan his retirement. Verses 18-19 tell us: *Then he said, 'This is what I'll do. I will tear down my barns and build bigger ones, and there I will store all my grain and my goods. 19 And I'll say to myself, "You have plenty of good things laid up for many years. Take life easy; eat, drink and be merry."* His attitude seems reasonable because it would be a waste not to provide for his surplus, but Jesus said that this man was a fool, not because of his goals, but because his goals ignored God. He says in verse 20, *"You fool! This very night your life will be demanded from you. Then who will get what you have prepared for yourself?'* (NIV)

We look at those who have a lot and assume they're happy and at those who have little and assume they're unhappy. The great deception of money and things is in thinking that in them are found the quality and quantity of life, that life is made up and measured by our possessions. This man assumed that he would have many years (quantity) to enjoy his many things (quality). This assumption was his deception. This deception is that money can do for us what only God can do. God alone is the Creator and Sustainer of life. This is why Jesus warns His listeners at the onset of this parable. *Watch out! Be on your guard against all kinds of greed; life does not consist in an abundance of possessions. Luke 12: 15 (NIV)*

# PLEASURES OF LIFE

Pleasure is a powerful thing. Powerful men have been toppled by a single night of pleasure. Kingdoms have been destroyed by their king's desire for pleasure. Just as it is human nature to avoid pain, it is also human nature to move toward pleasure. Both can be destructive. Just like a person who avoids the pain of chemotherapy may die of cancer, the person who is driven by pleasure can be manipulated by others. Pleasure can be the carrot on the stick that others may use to lead to our demise.

Pleasure can also be confused as needs. What do you really need? I would make an argument that coffee is a need, specifically Starbucks whole bean espresso roast coffee (this guy knows too much about coffee). You may say Coke or Pepsi are needs of your life. All we really need is water. Most everything else we drink is pleasure. Pleasure is produced from our ability to choose and having many choices from which to choose. Our grocery stores would be pretty small if all they provided for was our needs. I would conjecture that our whole American economy would collapse if all Americans woke up one morning and started purchasing just what they needed. I guess then Christmas would just have to be about Christ.

> *It does not diminish God in the least for us to ignore Him; it does, however, hurt us.*

Don't misunderstand me. God is not opposed to pleasure. He did not create a black and white, one-dimensional world. He created a world to meet our needs and give us pleasure. Like parents who enjoy watching their children open presents at Christmas, God enjoys giving and watching us open the good things of life. The problem is when the pleasures of life become our purpose for living to the exclusion of the Giver.

Something would be missing from Christmas morning if children opened all their presents and completely ignored their parents with no hug, no thank you, not even an acknowledgement of their presence and provision. If this is how children would handle the special gifts and pleasures of life, what would they do when their everyday needs were met? This lack of acknowledgement and appreciation is a sign of a spoiled child. God does not need our accolades, praise, appreciation, or even recognition. It does not diminish Him in the least for us to ignore Him; it does, however, hurt us. God meets our needs and gives us pleasure so that we might know and understand Him. God wants humanity to know His nature and character, so He gives us His world with all its provisions and pleasures, His love, and His kindness. Like children who suffer from the absence of parents, we suffer when we ignore our God. Just like children knowing and interacting with healthy parents make healthy adults, our knowing and interacting with God makes us healthy, mature human beings. Healthy people know the difference between needs and pleasures and are thankful to the One that meets both.

The God that created a world to provide for our needs and give us pleasure never intended for pleasures to be an end in themselves but a means to knowing and understanding Him. It is self-destructive when the desire for pleasure consumes our thoughts and the pursuit of pleasure devours our time, crowding out insight into the Giver of all things.

## CHAPTER 23: TRANSFORMATIVE PROCESS

Ever had surgery? What if you are in your room awaiting an appendectomy and a young doctor enters your room, claiming to be your surgeon, and says, "I just want you to know I read all the books on this procedure and in class made straight 'A's'"? At this point, are you going to let this doctor be your surgeon? I hope not! Let's go a little further. This time this same surgeon enters your room and says, "I was not only a straight "A" student, but I also have observed this surgery many times and can see myself performing this procedure on you." Are you ready to let him cut on you? Probably not. Let's try this again. This same doctor comes and adds to his previous resume of good grades and personal observation, "I care about you and your problem and really believe that this surgery will help. I want to help you." Is a knowledgeable, observant, caring doctor enough for you to allow this guy to put you under the knife and remove parts of you? Although it is closer to what you desire in your surgeon, I would bet it is still not enough. Allow me to add one last component to this scenario This time this young doctor comes into your room and, in addition to grades,

observation, and caring, adds, "Oh yes, I have done this procedure many times successfully." Would you allow this young doctor to do the procedure on you at this point? I would say probably so, unless you know something I do not.

Although the last scenario won you over, it is the whole thing that is really important. Surgery is a big deal. We want the guy who has all the knowledge medical school can provide proven by good grades. We want a doctor who has observed and can see himself performing this procedure. In addition, we want a doctor who cares about us. Finally, we want a doctor who has demonstrated competence. When all four of these come together, the doctor's character changes for us, and he is no longer A surgeon—he is now MY SURGEON. So we can see from this illustration how knowledge, perspective, conviction, and competence are key processes in character development. It is through this process that the young man I now call my surgeon has traveled. It is what turned him into my doctor and my surgeon.

Have you ever had a new job or engaged a new profession? Of course, if you are of any age, you probably have. After being hired and before you started, did you ever wake up at night, as I have, in a cold sweat thinking, "What am I doing? I have never done this before." Maybe you were filled with a degree of self-doubt asking yourself, "Can I really do this?" Except for the ignorant soul who, because he has done nothing, thinks he can anything, most of us have felt at least some degree of insecurity as we entered a new job that required a new skill set. This feeling probably drove you to get as much information as you could. You took manuals home to read—you watched training videos. You did anything that would increase your understanding of this new area of responsibility. If you could find someone who had done this job before, you picked their brain for any jewel of knowledge they could offer. As you gained more and more knowledge and understanding, you got greater insight into your job. This developed insight gave you perspective. With greater perspective came confidence or a feeling that you could do it. It was this feeling or conviction that led you to doing more, or competence. Finally, the more you did a job, the more competent you became and the more you could lay claim to being a professional. If you look at this from the side of your employer, the professional skills this process created are what they are paying you for. As a matter of fact, chances are your employer evaluated you in regards to these same 5 areas before they hired you.

I have used these two illustrations to help us understand the common nature of this process. For years I have used this in my ministry encounters to disciple, train, and counsel. Knowledge that leads to perspective, that leads to conviction, that leads to competence, that becomes character is a basic learning process. The relationship I have with God through the sacrifice of Christ is a free gift, but it must be opened and applied before we can truly say we are Christ-like. Using the Bible, the Holy Spirit, and the discipler, God wants us to know what He knows, to see as He sees, to feel as He feels, and to do what He does, so that we are as He is, not gods but godly children of our Father, living worthy of the name we have been given by grace—Christian. In my previous book, I wrote:

*This process permeates every sphere of an encounter, from the individual to the group, for the purpose of moving people from knowing to doing to being. This process works with the Holy Spirit as individuals read the word of God and as Christians learn to rightly handle the word of truth, from knowledge through application to incorporation into character. It is holistic, integrating the head (intellect) and heart (passions, emotions, and desires) and the hands and feet (behaviors). – Transformative Church Planting Movement*

I have done this process with many individuals and have found that those who have been Christians for years have already learned to do this. They know the stories of the Bible and will quickly move to perspective. With a little probing, they will then move to conviction and competence. What is natural, however, to an experienced Christian is not for a novice or even a non-Christian. This is why this process is so important. Knowledge the leads to transformation can be caught and taught. Like many educational tools, this process takes what is automatic for a Christian and breaks it down into repeatable steps that can be taught to the inexperienced.

## CHAPTER 24: WHAT DOES THE TRANSFORMATIVE PROCESS LOOK LIKE?

### KNOWLEDGE

The transformative process begins with knowledge. All learning curves start here. It is the foundation of growth and development in all areas of life; it is the facts, truths, and information we need to begin. As in my previous illustration, just because you have the knowledge of medical school does not mean you are a doctor. On the other hand, you cannot be a doctor without the knowledge of medical school.

So then, the first step in the transformative process is to help the disciple grow in his knowledge of scripture. Your job as the discipler is to guide the disciple as he engages this process. At this level questions are asked about the information of the passage. You ask them to tell you, "What are the facts?" If it's a narrative, ask them to tell you the story of the passage. Telling what you have read solidifies, deepens, and helps move them toward perspective. The leader is there to make sure the story that is told is correct and contains all the important information to build to the next level. Of course, different types of biblical literature require different questions. To explore knowledge of the epistles, a leader might ask them to paraphrase, asking, "In your own words, tell me what the writer is saying."

*Who, what, when, where* and *how* are information explorers. Although they can be used at other levels, at this level they are just used to clarify facts. *Who* identifies the characters. *What* explores the situation and circumstances. *When* is about timing of the events. *Where* defines the location. *How* investigates the methodology and motives of the characters. *Who is speaking? To whom is he speaking? What is the occasion? Where did all this happen? How did it come to be?* These are all valid questions to investigate and explore the facts of a passage.

### PERSPECTIVE

*Jesus did not speak to inform—He spoke to transform. When knowledge becomes personal, it produces perspective. Perspective is evaluating beyond the facts for the purpose of application. Knowledge looks at what the passage meant while perspective is what it means to me. – Transformative Church Planting Movement*

I remember as a child visiting my mother's family in Leakesville, Mississippi, a community so small that we walked everywhere, even to Sunday church. I had always remembered our walk to church as long and passing through a steep ravine. Years later, while visiting family, I walked to church and found the walk to be only a few short blocks and the ravine to be only a small slope. What changed? Well, I did. I grew up (outwardly anyway). With physical growth came a new perspective of Leakesville, Mississippi; what was once large, deep, and wide became small, shallow, and narrow. Greater maturity always brings new perspectives. This is true in life and in spiritual matters.

The God of the universe who sees all things as they really are wants us to see things as they really are, not just from our immature, limited perspective. He desires His children to have a continually renewed perspective that comes from hanging out with Him. As we spend time with Him, He takes the knowledge of His Word and uses it to expand our horizons and give us a vaster, more mature perspective. As a result, what once was overwhelming is now easily overcome, what at one time stressed us out is now insignificant. The big is now little, the deep is now shallow, and the wide is now narrow, all because God changed us, matured us, and gave us better perspective.

In regards to perspective, let's consider the parable of the sower found in Matthew 13, where Jesus describes the hard soil as not perceiving the truth of God's Word, with individuals not being willing to move beyond the facts.

*Matthew 12:19 (NIV) When anyone hears the message about the kingdom and does not understand it, the evil one comes and snatches away what was sown in his heart.*

The word *understand* literally means to put together, to bring together, or to metaphorically bring together ideas beyond the facts, to perceive or understand. This is perspective and it happens when knowledge becomes personal. At this level, we begin to see how information and knowledge work around us, in us, and through us. Evaluation and thoughts of application are major parts of perspective.

In this passage Jesus warns that hearing information that does not lead to understanding will be snatched away by the devil. All information and knowledge has an expiration date, and if it is not internalized, it will be taken away. If you don't use it, you will lose it. Jesus' audience was made up of at least two groups: those who were followers and those who were NOT followers. The followers assumed that there was more to the story and inquired about the deeper meaning beyond the facts while the others just heard a story about a farmer. The followers of Jesus assumed the authority of His teaching was from God and the direction of His teaching was for their benefit while those who were not followers questioned His authority and thought very little about His message. Thus, in the

> **While knowledge of the Bible will help us know about God, perspective will help us know HIM.**

words of Jesus: *In them is fulfilled the prophecy of Isaiah: "You will be ever hearing but never understanding; you will be ever seeing but never perceiving"* (Matthew 13:14 NIV).

I have come to believe in the 36/96 rule, which goes something like this: without reinforcement, information retention decays so that in 36 hours 96% will be forgotten. Check me out. On Wednesday in any church meeting, hand out a sheet of blank paper and have people who attended Sunday write everything they remember from the message. The 4% that is remembered will often be minor points, humorous comments, or generally insignificant details.

How do we turn knowledge into perspective? Ask questions about meaning. While knowledge is concerned about what it meant in the context of that day, perspective is concerned about what it means to me today. Included in perspective would be evaluation and exploring possible applications. At this level, questions are asked to explore personal insight that is built on the facts of a passage. While knowledge identifies the characters, perspective seeks characters to identify with.

If theology is the study of God, then the Bible exists to help us understand Him, not just intellectually but personally. While knowledge of the Bible will help us know about God, perspective will help us know HIM. Knowledge stops at the bottom of the mountain and looks up, while perspective is at the top looking down. We seek not our limited perspective but the view of God. Our desire is to see ourselves, others, and God Himself as God sees.

## CONVICTION

*If the whole process was a see saw, on one end you would have knowledge and perspective while on the other end you would have competence and character. In the middle, as the fulcrum, would be conviction. Conviction is the pivot point of change and transformation. – Transformative Church Planting Movement*

*When you can't make them see the light, make them feel the heat* is a quote attributed to Ronald Reagan. The truth is most of humanity will not make any significant change until they feel the heat. For some reason, just switching on the light of knowledge is met with little more than an appreciation for illumination with no real change. Knowledge and even a healthy perspective is not enough to move us out of the darkness into the light. We must feel the need to move. Strong feelings have often been the catalysts for big movements and change. MADD (Mothers Against Drunk Driving) and AMBER Alerts all come from people with strong feelings.

> **Riding the God-given wave of feelings produced by knowledge and perspective, you can help them see and form the motivation for the changes God desires.**

Most big changes in our lives are punctuated by strong feelings. I did not marry my wife just because it was a good idea, although it was (for me, maybe not for her). I married her because I also felt love for her and was infatuated with her. I have a picture taken by my mother of the first time they met Karen (probably as proof that I had a girlfriend). Whenever I look at that picture, I remember the event in detail because of the feelings I had for Karen, and it was not long after this that I asked her to marry me.

The same God who created intellect and reason also created emotions. Many parables and stories in the Bible were designed to evoke feelings to promote change. King David, after his affair with Bathsheba and an elaborate cover up that included arranging the death of her husband, is confronted by Nathan the prophet. Nathan does not just recite the facts of God's case against David; he tells him a story specifically designed to get David to feel the consequences of his behavior.

*2 Samuel 12:1–15 (NIV) The LORD sent Nathan to David. When he came to him, he said, "There were two men in a certain town, one rich and the other poor. 2 The rich man had a very large number of sheep and cattle, 3 but the poor man had nothing except one little ewe lamb he had bought. He raised it, and it grew up with him and his children. It shared his food, drank from his cup and even slept in his arms. It was like a daughter to him. 4 "Now a traveler came to the rich man, but the rich man refrained from taking one of his own sheep or cattle to prepare a meal for the traveler who had come to him. Instead, he took the ewe lamb that belonged to the poor man and prepared it for the one who had come to him." 5 David burned with anger against the man and said to Nathan, "As surely as the LORD lives, the man who did this deserves to die! 6 He must pay for that lamb four times over, because he did such a thing and had no pity." 7 Then Nathan said to David, "You are the man!...13 Then David said to Nathan, "I have sinned against the Lord."*

Nathan's story so penetrates the heart of this former shepherd boy that, burning with anger, King David pronounces a judgment on the culprit in the story. Nathan then seizes the opportunity that David's anger presents and identifies David as the culprit, proclaiming, *"You are the man!"* In an instant David is broken, his anger turns to grief, and his grief turns to repentance.

Using the perspective that comes from knowledge, we can inductively help move the person to conviction. You may start with identifying the emotions revealed in the passage by asking, "How do you think he/she/they felt?" Because motives are often closely linked to feelings, you may ask, "What motive can you identify in this passage?" or "What are the motives of the characters?" You may also ask, "How do you think the person felt? What are the emotions expressed in the passage?" before more directly asking, "How do YOU feel about this truth God has revealed to you?"

Many times feelings are revealed in their perspectives. For example, after reading the story of the Woman at the Well in John 4, the person might say, "I really identify with this woman and feel that Jesus went out of His way to engage me, too." The response to this could be, "Well, tell me more about how this makes you feel." As they explore their feelings, you are looking for the ones you can build upon.

Feeling may vary from passage to passage and from person to person. The person in above example, after identifying with the woman, may express joy and gratitude. Another person may look at this story and, as a Christian, feel guilt because, unlike Jesus, they are unwilling to engage certain people because of their bias and prejudice. Riding the God-given wave of feelings produced by knowledge and perspective, you can help them see and form the motivation for the changes God desires. Some feelings may set a new course of scripture reading. For example, someone who continually feels condemnation in spite of the progress you see in their life may need to stop their present reading and start reading passages about God's love and forgiveness.

Let me remind you that these feelings come from the perspective that the Holy Spirit has given this person, based on the truth of God's Word. These feelings are pivotal and form the motivation for doing that leads to being. These feelings will prompt them to build competence that leads to character. The discipler's job is to identify the feelings that will be the catalyst for the next step in transformation.

## COMPETENCE

*Competence is doing something about what we know, see, and feel. "Practice makes perfect" does not just apply to learning a new skill, it is also literally the way that God transforms us. When we know and see things the way that God knows and sees them and really feel about things the way that He does, we are compelled to do whatever He desires – Transformative Church Planting Movement*

As a gymnast in high school and college, I learned the value of improving skills through repetition. The knowledge that comes from learning the techniques behind a skill, the perspective that comes from watching others perform the skill, the conviction that comes from knowing how to do it and seeing how it is done all led me to one thing—doing it for the first time. Now, I am not an idiot. Often, the first time meant a lot of thick mats, spotting belts, and spotters (people to catch you). After the first time, and if you were still alive, came more instruction (knowledge), personal insight (perspective), greater confidence (conviction), and a 2nd attempt. A good example of this is a skill that I developed in high school gymnastics called a standing back flip. After going through this process and having done 1000s of these, this skill stayed with me until I was in my 30's. Yes, as a church planter/pastor, a kid would come to me on Sunday morning after church and ask me to do a standing back flip, and in my dress shoes, suit, and tie, I would do one for him. I stopped in my thirties not because the skill left me but because my muscles did. I knew it was time to stop when, after finishing it, my nose was 4" from the ground. The spirit was willing but the flesh became weak. The point that I am making is that just like practicing riding a bike or, for me, doing a back-flip creates proficiency, spiritual practice can make perfect or mature, proficient followers of Jesus Christ.

Jesus Himself, after His teaching in the Sermon on the Mount, stated the importance of putting His words into practice.

*Matthew 7: 24-27 (NIV) "Therefore everyone who hears these words of mine and puts them into practice is like a wise man who built his house on the rock. 25 The rain came down, the streams rose, and the winds blew and beat against that house; yet it did not fall, because it had its foundation on the rock. 26 But everyone who hears these words of mine and does not put them into practice is like a foolish man who built his house on sand. 27 The rain came down, the streams rose, and the winds blew and beat against that house, and it fell with a great crash." 28 When Jesus had finished saying these things, the crowds were amazed at his teaching, 29 because he taught as one who had authority, and not as their teachers of the law.*

Listening with an attitude that leads to actions produces transformation. When we build our lives upon the rock of God's Word, i.e., hearing that anticipates, plans, and aligns with its truth, it creates a life that will stand through difficult times. This implementing of God's Word changes us, not the things around us. It does not prevent the storms; it just gives us the foundation to withstand them. It does not reduce a storm's force from a category 5 to a Category 3; it changes me so that I may endure it. It is this enduring life that stand as a proof to all that faith in God works. The same storms that wash away the foundations of those who trust in other things is the storm that affirms my faith in God and others. We will not weather the storm just because we attend church and hear the Word or because we faithfully read it but because it gets in us and changes us. It penetrates and permeates our lives in such a way that it is seen in our behavior. It is the Word of God that goes in, on, and down, developing roots that sustain, and then up, producing fruit that remains.

> *Helping others to build competence requires healthy accountability that makes others responsible for the application of revealed truth.*

Hearing with doing in mind: this is an interesting thought. It is often the difference between training and school. In school, kids are taught the basics. Most children and teenagers do not have a clue what they will be doing in life; therefore, math, science, and English are taught foundationally to build upon later. This is why they will often ask, "When will I ever use this?" Honestly, our answer should be, "I don't know. It really depends on what you do with your life." I am not saying that these basics are not important. They must be learned because kids do not know what they are going to do. Because they do not see a direct connection between what they are learning and real life, they do not listen with an attitude of doing. On the other hand, the guy taking on a new job goes through his training listening to every word with an attitude of doing. He knows there is a direct connection between life or his livelihood and what he is learning.

Jesus in the passage above is talking about listening with doing in mind. In essence, the wise person listens to the words of Jesus assuming they have meaning and plan to do something about it while the unwise (that would be the foolish person) listens to Jesus but sees no authority in His Word and is unwilling to consider its practical application.

Helping others to build competence requires healthy accountability that makes others responsible for the application of revealed truth. As God's Word moves from knowledge to perspective, which is used by the Spirit to bring conviction, we must be ready to ask hard questions about behavior and practices. In the area of competence, *who, what, when,* and *where* are used to point others in the direction of conduct and in the application of this truth that has been revealed. What will you do with this truth? Who will hold you accountable as you implement this truth? What do you need to do differently? When will you report on your progress? Where will you report your progress? How can I support you in this? How can I hold you accountable? How can I pray for you?

## THE RESULT: CHRIST-LIKE CHARACTER

*Consistently doing what we know and feel produces character. Godly character--Christlikeness--comes from hanging out with Him through prayer and His Word, knowing what He knows, seeing like He sees, feeling like He feels, doing what He does, and being like He is. God has given us the Bible and His Spirit so we might know, see, feel, do, and be like Christ. Jesus never taught for intellectual stimulation; He always taught for transformation, i.e., Christ-like character development. – Transformative Church Planting Movement*

When all is said and done, this process should bring about internal change that should be seen in outward behavior. The measurement of this is Jesus Christ. Remember, Jesus came to earth not just to give His life but to give OF His life. As the perfect God, He was the perfect sacrifice for our sins, but as God in the flesh, He was the perfect example of a follower of God. He is the measure of success for a Christian. As we engage the Bible, we need to know what He knows, so that we might see as He sees, so that we might feel as He feels, leading us to do what He does, in order to be like HE is. Once again, let me repeat the mantra of the book:

*Transformation happens when you get an individual into the Word in such a way that gets the Word into them so that they become like The Word – Jesus Christ.*

While the last two sections have dealt with the process of getting people into the Bible and getting the truth of God's Word into people, the next section will address this measurement of being and becoming like Christ.

# SECTION 4: CHRISTLIKENESS: THE CHRISTIAN'S MEASURE OF SUCCESS

## CHAPTER 25: DEFINING SPIRITUAL MATURITY: THE IDEAL OF JESUS

Christ loved to hang out with His Heavenly Father to talk with Him and listen to Him. They were in constant communion with one another. In this way and in every way, Jesus formed the ideal of being a Christian. He is the measurement of maturity. We are to work toward being like Christ or our ideal elder brother and Lord. Paul, in the passage below, teaches us that Jesus is the measurement of the church, both individually and corporately. He states that it is the purpose of leadership to train Christians to be like Christ. This maturity measured by Christlikeness will be demonstrated in fewer distractions (not being tossed back in forth) and greater effectiveness (as each does its part).

*Ephesians 4:11 So Christ himself gave the apostles, the prophets, the evangelists, the pastors and teachers, 12 to equip his people for works of service, so that the body of Christ may be built up 13 until we all reach unity in the faith and in the knowledge of the Son of God and become mature,* **attaining to the whole measure of the fullness of Christ.** *14 Then we will no longer be infants, tossed back and forth by the waves, and blown here and there by every wind of teaching and by the cunning and craftiness of people in their deceitful scheming. 15 Instead, speaking the truth in love,* **we will grow to become in every respect the mature body of him who is the head, that is, Christ.** *16 From him the whole body, joined and held together by every supporting ligament, grows and builds itself up in love, as each part does its work.*

"In the beginning was the Word or *Logos*" (Greek) is the way that John, the disciple who leaned on Jesus and the only one to follow Him all the way to the cross, chose to start his book. As you look at the Greek word *logos*, you might say that Jesus was the *logo* of God. Now for those who are concerned about proper exegesis here, I am using *logo* as an illustration, more than a translation or interpretation of the word *logos*. Just as a logo is a visual expression of a business or entity, Jesus was the expression of God on earth. He communicated, like a logo, who God is and what He stands for. If you want to know what God is like, look at Jesus' life and teaching. John tells us that Jesus, The Word, became flesh and dwelt or took up residence among humanity. He adds that in Jesus we beheld the glory of God's one and only Son. What is interesting is that throughout the first chapter of John there are only two references to Jesus' death. The rest of the chapter and book is about Jesus revealing God to humanity. It is about the life, ministry, and teaching of Jesus. While the death and resurrection are essential, John starts and spends most of his book telling us about how Jesus dwelt among us.

We spend a lot of time in church talking about the death, burial, and resurrection of Christ but neglect the fact that He spent 33 years getting there. What was the purpose of those 33 years prior to the events that paid the price for humanity? While Jesus, God in the flesh, could have died at any time providing the perfect sacrifice for our forgiveness, why 33 years? The answer is simple but often overlooked by Christians in their everyday life. You see, Christ not only came to die for our sins, He also came to show us how to live for God. He was the second Adam who got it right. He is the new prototype for a new man. While apart from His death, burial, and resurrection we could not live for God, we must also realize that living for God is why Christ gave His life. Jesus lived to show us how a person totally surrendered to God should live.

> Christ not only came to die for our sins, He also came to show us how to live for God.

One of the problems Christians face is the idea of living up to the example of the perfect Lord. Although we will never be perfect, we are perfectionists of one kind or another. For all of the groups, perfection is still the standard. The difference is in what they do with the standard. Some people are so overwhelmed by the perfect model of Jesus that they simply don't try. These perfectionists see perfection as not just unattainable but completely unapproachable and, therefore, show little or no interest in doing better or engaging in any form of improvement. "No one is perfect. Why should I try?" is their motto. In the extremes of this attitude, you would find hedonism and a life of excess.

"No one is perfect, but I will try," is the motto of the next group of perfectionists. They live a very strict life in their efforts to attain what is more than excellent—perfection. These perfectionists believe that perfection is not only approachable but also attainable and, therefore, live life continually disappointed by their efforts. For those apart from Christ and many who are in Christ, these seem to be the only two options. Either they don't try at all or they try without God.

The third alternative is seeing Jesus as the ideal. Ideal means that Jesus is the perfect example for us to follow. Although not attainable on this earth, Jesus' example is approachable through God's work of sanctification. The world is full of idols that are not ideal, examples that are far from perfect which if imitated are disappointing and unsatisfactory. The right ideal can inspire while the wrong ideal can be limiting. One problem of our society is that we have lowered the ideal. The news is full of stories of the rich and famous whose lives appear to be picturesque. There are stories of beautiful people who find, fall in love with, and marry beautiful people. "Oh, if I could only be like them" is the prayer of many. It is only later, with time that tests the quality of all relationships, that we find the lives of these American idols have become train wrecks filled with drug addictions, alcohol abuse, failed marriages, and broken families. If this weren't true, then the tabloids would have nothing to write about. These are often the idyllic models that so many will attempt to emulate, never realizing that using worldly standards will give only worldly results. This ideal manufactured by money and fame is the best our world can produce in its present fallen state, but there is another way, a new ideal—Jesus. Jesus came to raise the bar, show us a new way to live, and give us the way to reach it. Though His life, we see a way that we might live (the ideal), and through His death, we see the avenue He provided for us to achieve it. If I could flip a switch and in one instant produce in the heart of every person the love for God and others described in the great commandment, wouldn't that be wonderful? Wouldn't that be IDEAL? We can live a life like this. We can love God with all our heart, soul, and mind and our neighbors as ourselves because Jesus showed us how.

# CHAPTER 26: TEST OF SPIRITUAL MATURITY: BEING LIKE JESUS

I am afraid of tests, probably because of all the ones I have failed, but tests are good when you see them not as pass or fail but as an evaluation of progress. This makes the tests I take about me and my progress, and from the test, I can learn what needs to be addressed so that I may do better. I wish I had understood this in school. Testing for evaluation is why God often allows and even ordains difficult situations and people in my life. As in Peter's denial, Jesus knew that Peter was full of himself, lacked integrity, and was hypocritical in that his actions would not match his words. God allowed Peter to be tested, not so God would know, but so Peter might know and evaluate his relationship with God.

Let's take a test to see if your words match your life and to see if you are a grown-up or growing Christian. Consider each question carefully and honestly.

1. Like Jesus, I am constantly in communication with God. Several times a day I feel the need to stop and pray about situations and people I encounter.
2. Like Jesus, I love to get into God's Word. I have regular conversations about what I am reading in the Bible. I read the Bible with anticipation of God speaking to me.
3. Like Jesus, I see the value of relationships with others. Supporting others and being supported by them is natural and makes me happy. Because I am still on this journey to be more like Christ, my support includes talking to others about holding me accountable for the changes God has revealed to me through His Word.
4. Like Jesus, I grieve over lostness. I feel a sense of loss for those around me who do not have the kind of relationship with God that I do.
5. Like Jesus, I celebrate the things that really matter. I think less about physical things and more about heavenly things. I see the meeting of my needs as God's provision and the extra things as God's gifts. I see all I have as tools to be used for God's kingdom and not my benefit.
6. Like Jesus, I am righteous. Although my righteousness is imputed righteousness, which is a product of God's forgiveness, I sin less and there less in my life to forgive. My character is changing for the better each year. I enjoy talking to others about the truth of God's Word and the changes it makes in me.
7. Like Jesus, I love God and others. I love more than I used to. I see engaging the Word and prayer as spending time with God to know Him more intimately and personally, and as I do, I express more love toward Him and others.
8. Like Jesus, I am sometimes criticized and belittled for my relationship with God. At times people hate me just because I am a follower of Jesus.
9. Like Jesus, I am light to people. People notice the changes in my life and would say that I am a better person than I used to be, more like Christ. Because of this God-given influence, many of these individuals allow me to spiritually speak into their life.

# CHAPTER: 27: MOTIVATION FOR SPIRITUAL MATURITY: THE BENEFITS OF CHRISTIANITY

"Lord, break me" is a phrase I have heard prayed many times by people with tremendous sincerity. While they are praying this as an expression of their desire for God to remove all the obstacles to fellowship with Him, it has still always made me feel uncomfortable. I would rather pray, "Lord, keep me in a place where you do not have to break me." I would rather be motivated by appreciation for God's love and grace than by fear of His wrath. I would rather remain malleable in the Potter's hands than be broken by them. Being motivated by appreciation for the many benefits of the relationship we have with God is being Christ-like. While the fear of the Lord is the beginning of wisdom (Prov. 9:10), perfect, mature love casts out all fear (1 John 4:18).

In a previous chapter, I wrote about love replacing fear and how most adult children can relate to this transition as they lovingly care for their aging parents. Now allow me share with you where this idea first hit me. One day, while sitting around the table with my children as we were discussing our upcoming trip to Texas to visit my parents, I saw a teachable moment. I asked my children why they thought I did things for my parents when I was a boy. They replied, "Because if you didn't, you would get in trouble." I responded, "So I did it because I was afraid." I then asked them, "Why do you think I do things for them today? Am I afraid that your grandfather might spank me or your grandmother might ground me?" "NO," they replied, laughing at this absurdity. Then I asked, "Why do I do what my parents ask me to do today?" Christopher, my son, responded in a questioning tone, "Because you love them?" I then spent the next few minutes (hours in kid time) telling them about how and why my motivation for service to my parents changed from fear to love, from dread to joy. I attempted to communicate to them that today I see all the things my parents did for me while I was growing up and realize that I could never repay them for the sacrifice they made for their children. I told my children that I look forward to doing things for my parents as a token of appreciation for all they have done for me.

> The Christian life should be lived as a token of appreciation for the overwhelming, undeserved grace and mercy we have been and are continually given.

This is the motivation that God desires of us toward Him. The Christian life should be lived as a token of appreciation for the overwhelming, undeserved grace and mercy we have been and are continually given. Oh, that we might serve God out of loving gratitude for all He has given us. Is not this what Paul is talking about when he says in Roman 12:1, "In view of the mercies of God, offer your body a living sacrifice"? In other words, in light of all God has done for us, shouldn't we respond by offering all we are? Aren't you glad that God says "living sacrifice" since most sacrifices are dead? It is in the context of the forgiveness that comes from the great mercy God has given us in Christ that we now offer ourselves as a token of thanksgiving.

## Intimacy the Measure of Jesus

When I look into my wife's eyes and tell her that she is the only one for me, she does not want to know I am faithful to her only because of obedience to God's command. She does not want to know the reason I do not cheat on her is the investment I have made in her and our children. NO. Although all of these are good reasons for my faithfulness, my wife wants to know that I do not violate my vows to her because I love her, uniquely her. She wants to know that to break her heart would break my heart, to violate her trust would violate me, to cheat on her would be cheating on me. Oh, that the next husband to engage pornography would feel the betrayal, the next man that gets on the Ashley Madison website would feel the pain that it causes their spouse. You would have to be pretty close to someone to feel their pain. You would have to really know them as a person to share in their suffering. This would be intimacy

When my wife was being prepped for the birth of our son, I found myself intrigued by the whole medical environment. I observed with detachment like a professional as they injected the I.V. into her hand. When it slipped out, I was clinically amazed how the tissue under the skin filled with blood. Then as I looked up to inform my wife of my observation (the woman who almost did not marry me because of the required blood test) and as her head turned toward me and away from the procedure, I noticed a tear rolling down her cheek. This small tear was her only expression of pain. In a blink of an eye, "the clinician" in me turned into Karen's husband and my knees became weak, my head light, and my skin clammy. It was as if they had stuck me, and I had to sit down before I fell down (men don't faint). The tear reminded me that this was bone of my bone and flesh of my flesh and that the two of us were one. This was not an intellectual response but an emotional one. These feelings were not planned—they were natural—they were my instinctive response to her pain. It is a product of intimacy that comes from years of marriage (now 30+), not just living together, but growing together, experiencing life together. For over 30 years, Karen and I have been physically, emotionally, and spiritually intimate. They were not just hurting my best friend; they were hurting a part of me. Because of this intimacy, hers is the only mind that I can read with a high degree of accuracy, and in most situations, I could tell you what she is thinking and how she feels. Intimacy means she knows my needs and desires and I know hers, and we work together to see that they are met. .

God desires, has provided, and wants to share in this kind of intimacy with us. He knows how to be close to someone. Let's face it. You cannot get any closer than Father, Son, and Holy Spirit: three in one. The whole idea of the Trinity, as confusing as it is, represents wonderful intimacy. Jesus expresses His desire that we have this kind of relationship in His prayer for us to His Father.

*John 17: 20-21 (NIV) I do not ask on behalf of these alone, but for those also who believe in Me through their word; 21 that they may all be one; even as You, Father, are in Me and I in You, that they also may be in Us, so that the world may believe that You sent Me.*

John understood this intimacy perhaps better than any other man on earth. He is the one who leaned on Jesus. Let's face it: it seems kind of creepy for men to think of one man leaning on another man. Want to see a man's fight or flight response kick in? Next time you're at church sitting next to your hunting buddy, just lean into him as a gesture of intimacy and see how he reacts. Yes, it's creepy, until you put it in the context of a small boy sleeping in the lap his father or a teenager boy and his 4 year old brother leaning next to him as they watch TV. Intimacy like this, even to a man, is normal and even expected. I can remember times in my life when my father put his arms around me to comfort and affirm me. I remember times between my son and me where as men, we have wept together. While most affection between my son and me is expressed with punches, shoving, and head slaps, there have been times when, after a long conversation at a difficult time in his life, he hugged me so tight that I thought my eyes would pop out. I liked it so much that I attempted to make his eyes pop out. I think God likes it, too. He enjoys it when real men of any age surrender to the arms of their divine big Brother and eternal Father, *as You, Father, are in Me and I in You, that they also may be in Us, so that the world may believe that You sent Me.*

It is in the intimacy of this oneness that we become real men and true witnesses to the world. Intimacy with God and others, produced in us by Jesus, is the measure of a Christian.

# SECTION 5: MAINTAINING GROWTH WITH INTEGRITY

## CHAPTER 28: KEEP IT PERSONAL, SIMPLE, AND ORIGINAL

Just because people are theologically educated does not guarantee purity of their doctrine. We have had Bible colleges and seminaries for years, and yet we still have leadership emerging from our institutes who fall off the wagon of sound doctrine into the mire of unbiblical belief or heresy. In addition, regular attendance in church, including Bible Study, has not stopped the flow of bad practices in churches filled with good theology. I have personally been invited to help churches as they were experiencing a meltdown that ended with an exodus or split that could have been prevented if all the parties had loved one another as Christ loved the church and gave His life for it. This is not just in my tribe of churches. Church groups that strictly control the entry points and movement of their leadership do not fare any better when it comes to moral failure and church splits. A man-made system with all its checks and balances cannot guarantee the integrity of all its leadership or congregations.

Yes, ministry is risky; it always has been, but the benefits outweigh the risk. There is no perfect way to do this with imperfect people. We must stop trusting in our systems and processes and start trusting in God, His Word, and the ongoing work of the Holy Spirit. As I pull out old sermons and read them, I am amazed at some of the things I used to believe and am downright frightened by others. Through it all, however, God has done His work in me, through me, and sometimes in spite of me.

> *The integrity of any church begins with the integrity of the individual believers of the church.*

I say all this to address a question that I am often asked as I talk about developing a transformative culture, specifically by those who have read my first book *Transformative Church Planting Movement*. How do you protect the movement from cultism, heresy, stupidity, and bad practices? My answer is simple, "Well, I can't.... but God can." In 30+ years of ministry, I have tried to prevent the list above without much success. Today, I believe I know the reason. The problem with the church is not a lack of vision, it is not a lack of resources, it is not a lack of purpose: it is a lack of individual holiness. We have not sufficiently emptied the human vessels of clay before we have empowered them. We do not diagnose and deal with spiritual defects produced by sin before we determine spiritual giftedness and deploy them. True discipleship begins with denial before it moves to endowments. It ensures the journey of mercy before grace. Look at the following quote from *Transformative Church Planting Movement*.

*Mercy is God not giving us what we deserve while grace is God giving us far more than we ever deserve. Although they are two sides of the same coin, they are different. In God's mercy, He forgives me my sins and removes them from my life, and in His grace He gives me a home in heaven. In true discipleship, one must experience mercy, then grace. Just like a glass must be emptied before it can be filled, our lives must be purged of bad habits, our hang-ups, in order to be filled with the good things God desires to give. This is the process of sanctification or being made holy by God. How many times have pastors and church leaders empowered the talented only to be embarrassed later by hidden sins? People who experience real house-cleaning kind of mercy from God want to serve Him out of a heart of gratitude. Gratitude and love are the chief motives of a Christian and foundational for a transformative calling. – Transformative Church Planting Movement*

The integrity of any church begins with the integrity of the individual believers of the church. Focusing on the individual journey of believers maintains growth with integrity. Just like a healthy lawn is the best defense against weeds, spiritually healthy individuals who have been emptied of sin and are full of the Spirit are the best defense against heresy and bad practice.

Growth with integrity is also maintained by simplicity. Jesus did all the work of salvation for us. The Holy Spirit does the convicting or convincing of the lost. What is a Christian to do? What is our job? It is simple; we must continually surrender to the truth of God as He reveals it through His Word and the Holy Spirit. The transformative church culture centers on the primary source: the Word. It seeks the primary motivator and interpreter—the Holy Spirit—and seeks the simple mission of Christ. It uses simple, easily reproducible models and methods for making disciples.

Another aspect that will help maintain growth with integrity is to make copies from the original. If you have ever made a copy of a copy, you probably noticed that the copy is never quite as good as the original. If you continued to make a copy of a copy, it would, after many generations, be considerably degraded. The only way to maintain the integrity of the copies is to always copy from the original. The transformative culture is one that continually reproduces from the original, not a copy of a copy. One of the major problems of the Corinthian church was their attempt to copy from the copies. The development of the personality cults within the church, expressed by Paul as "I follow" Paul, Peter, Apollos, or Christ, was their attempt to pick favorites and debate what they saw as the philosophies of each. Those who identified themselves as the followers of Christ did so to the exclusion of the men that God had used to bring them the Gospel and to teach them the teachings of Christ while the others attempted to just copy from the copies of Christ. Paul started with his own personality cult and with a set of rhetorical questions attempted to get their focus back on Christ, the Original.

*1 Corinthians 1:11-13 (NIV) 11 My brothers and sisters, some from Chloe's household have informed me that there are quarrels among you. 12 What I mean is this: One of you says, "I follow Paul"; another, "I follow Apollos"; another, "I follow Cephas"; still another, "I follow Christ." 13 Is Christ divided? Was Paul crucified for you? Were you baptized in the name of Paul?*

This was the first attempt to denominationalize the church, focusing on the teachings of some of the followers of Jesus and pitting them against the teachings of other followers. This is interesting when you consider that most denominations come from or through the teachings of one man who was just trying to follow the teachings of the Bible. Although some religious leaders thought they had a corner on truth and intentionally started their group, other well-meaning leaders did so unintentionally. Some of these guys would be surprised at what their followers have done with their teachings. They would be shocked at how some of their personal practices and devotional habits have been canonized by these groups as essential theological tenets that divide and separate them from other Christians. Perhaps one reason the church is dying in America is that the traditions and rituals of men passed down and added onto throughout generations have blurred the original image of Christ and His teachings, to the point that they are almost unrecognizable to a lost and dying world.

The church does not exist to copy existing church models or leaders but to reproduce Christ in the lives of people. God has given us everything we need to copy from the original.

# CHAPTER 29: SIMPLE MANTRA FOR BETTER FOCUS

*Transformation happens when you get an individual into the Word in such a way that gets the Word into them so that they become like The Word – Jesus Christ.*

The simplicity of the mantra centering on the Word of God helps us keep our copies of Christ more Christ-like. Before it can be applied to others, each individual must ask, "Am I getting into the Word in a way that is getting the Word into me? Am I becoming like The Word – Jesus Christ?" What we are really talking about is John 15, where Jesus tells us about abiding or remaining in Him. Even in this passage the imagery is not about copying from a copy or a making a branch from another branch; it is about each individual maintaining his connection to Christ, the vine and the original.

*John 15:1-17 (NIV) 4 Remain in me, as I also remain in you. No branch can bear fruit by itself; it must remain in the vine. Neither can you bear fruit unless you remain in me. 5 "I am the vine; you are the branches. If you remain in me and I in you, you will bear much fruit; apart from me you can do nothing. 6 If you do not remain in me, you are like a branch that is thrown away and withers; such branches are picked up, thrown into the fire, and burned. 7 If you remain in me and my words remain in you, ask whatever you wish, and it will be done for you. 8 This is to my Father's glory, that you bear much fruit, showing yourselves to be my disciples.*

Growth with integrity begins with individuals who are abiding in Christ, who are in an intimate relationship with Him. You cannot engage the work of the Lord without abiding in the Lord of the work. Maintaining growth with integrity begins with personal maintenance. In begins with you and in you before it can flow through you. Abiding in Christ means staying connected to the source of our power and productivity. I am not just talking about the peace between God and man that comes from salvation; I am talking about maintaining continual peace that comes from abiding in Christ. The question is: how do we remain in a productive relationship with God?

> **You cannot be a disciple without discipline, and you cannot have discipline without disciplines in your life.**

## THE DISCIPLINE OF PRODUCTIVE BIBLE STUDY

"Devotions" and "Quiet Time" are phrases we use to describe our personal time with God, where we read the Bible and pray. Although setting time aside and engaging these practices are important, some Christians are doing this every day with little or no transformation taking place. According to Jesus, abiding means producing – bearing fruit. By fruit, does Jesus mean character or sharing our faith? Well, YES, both. Christ-like attitude always leads to Christ-like actions. Knowing should lead to doing, and consistent doing should lead to being, which leads to greater knowledge, deeper intimacy, doing, being, and so on... We should engage the Word so that, as Jesus commanded, it can teach us to obey everything He commanded (Mathew 28). I am not talking about reading the Word to tickle my intellect; I am talking about hearing from God to get my marching orders. We should read it as a soldier would read the orders from his commanding officer, as a lover would read the letters from his love, and as a patient would read the results of his test. We should get into it expecting it to get into us, anticipating a word from God, i.e., marching orders from our Commander-in-Chief. I would encourage you to go back in this book and look at the chapter entitled *The Transformative Culture: Learning to Listen*. This will help you to understand how studying God's Word in the morning sets you up to see Him at work all day long. This is abiding.

## THE DISCIPLINE OF EFFECTIVE PRAYER

Like electricity needs wires, Christians need prayer. It connects us to all God desires to do in us, to us, for us, and through us. As I get into God's word and as it gets into me, I quickly realize that God's plans are always bigger than I am. Through prayer God empowers me to accomplish what He has revealed through His Word for me to do. This means that if I am really hearing God speak, I mean really listening, it should continually drive me to my knees with an overwhelming sense of need. We should feel what Abraham felt when God told him to leave the comfort of his home without a map or destination, what Moses felt when God told him to go back to Egypt where he was a wanted man, or what Gideon felt when God whittled his army down to 300 men and told him to go and defeat the Midianite army of 150,000. When we get into God's word and it gets into us, prayer is our natural response.

In order to understand this, we must address a big misconception about prayer. Prayer does not put God into my sphere; it puts me into His. It does not engage God in my agenda; it places me into His. God's purposes and plans are like a flowing river—when we pray, we move into its flow. This does not mean God does not change things in us and around us. We can have impact through prayer, but nothing will change without God's permission or move beyond His sovereign plan.

In Matthew 6:9, Jesus tells us how we should pray to keep us in the flow of God. He tells His followers, "This is how you should pray." "How" was not a reference to the content of prayer but the attitude behind our prayer. Jesus, in the previous verses, had condemned showboating prayers and empty repetitive prayers, so why would we think that He was giving His followers a public, repetitive prayer? This "how you should pray" is about the faith or beliefs we must have in order to pray effectively. Faith is the attitude that reaches the altitude of God.

By faith, I mean the idea of trusting in, relying on, or having confidence in. I am not talking about more work; I am talking about less work. I am talking about stopping or ceasing your labor and relying on the work of God in and through you. Whether sitting in a chair or stepping onto a plane, there is a place where all our physical weight is transferred to that object. This is the kind of faith I mean: when we give up control and trust the chair to hold us up and the plane to get us to our destination. Because the purpose of this is to pray effectively to maintain integrity personally and in the transformative culture, I will briefly address these beliefs and then flesh them out in more detail in a later book. These are beliefs we must be hold dear to our heart to pray effectively. These are the truths that we must bring to the table in order to participate in the feast of God's power and plan.

## *The Intimacy of God: Our Father in Heaven*

To pray effectively we must trust in the intimacy of our God; we must relax in the relationship with our Father. God through Christ has given us the privilege of calling the God we worship "Father" (John 1:12) and, even more intimately, "Daddy" (Mark 14:36, Romans 8:4, Galatians 4:6). I have worked with many children in my 30+ years of ministry, but only three have the special right to call me "Daddy." This right gives them access to me, resources from me, and closeness to me that other children do not have; our relationship with our heavenly Father does the same for us. While my time is temporary, my resources are small, and my presence has limits, God our Father is eternal, His resources are endless, and His presence is limitless. Who's your DADDY NOW?

## *The Holiness of God: Hallowed be Your Name*

Although God our Father is accessible, is close, and desires intimacy with you, He is not one you can take for granted. While He, our heavenly Father, is somewhat like our earthly father, He is different, holy, set apart, and unique, and we must respect His holiness. Holiness implies uniqueness, set apart from another. Like a dishwasher, God accepts us when we are dirty with sin, cleans us up, and sets us apart for the unique use for which He created us. In regards to God, He is the dishwasher; He is the unique maker. *Holy (Hallowed) be your Name* refers the uniquely good nature and character of God that we must respect. He is holy, set apart, and objectively above it all.

## *The Reign of God: Your Kingdom come, your will be done on earth as it is in heaven*

We must trust in the greater good of God's kingdom. We must surrender to His personal reign and His desire to reign in others. No one would invite a kingdom to come and the will of a king to ensue unless they were his subjects in that kingdom. Effective prayer is trusting in and desiring God's reign on earth.

## *The Provision of God: Give us this day our daily bread.*

We must stop worrying about the things of this world and relax and trust in the provision of God. While bread is a side dish for us, it was the staple of the first century. If you did not have bread, you probably did not have food. To a first century Jew, "God, give us this day our daily bread" was equivalent to "God, meet my needs." Effective prayer sees God as the source of all provisions of life, physically and spiritually. Jesus who fed the 5000 in the beginning of John 6 is the same Jesus who said, "I am the bread of life," at the end of that same chapter.

*The Forgiveness of God: Forgive us our debts as we forgive our debtors.*

Effective prayer relaxes in the overwhelming mercy of God. We are so overwhelmed by God's mercy that showing forgiveness to others is easy. Effective prayer drives us to confession of sin and produces acceptance of others in spite of their sins.

*The Protection of God: Lead us not into temptation but deliver us from the evil one*

Effective prayer means trusting in the power of God's deliverance. We must trust Him to protect us from the devil and from his schemes to trap us.

When we pray like this, we are in the sweet spot of God's plan and, thus, more able to find the person of peace. All of these attitudes perfectly set us up for the discovery of the person of peace. As we pray, we move into the flow of God's plan, and with this attitude, we can move through our day with the confidence that He is at work in us and around us. Thus, we approach the people of our day with the attitude that our heavenly Father, who delivers us from temptation and sin, who forgive and fills our heart with a desire to forgive, who provides for all our needs, and who is like no other but wonderfully unique and set apart, wants to be their Father, too. With the confidence of having entered into His presence through prayer, I know every day as I approach others that He has prepared some to hear and respond to the Good News and that God can be their heavenly Father, too. Thus, prayer keeps me abiding in God's presence: the sweet spot of God's plan.

## CHAPTER 31: SIMPLE FRACTAL FOR MEASURING SUCCESS

*Fractals are all around us. Fractals are geometric shapes often non-regular that have the same shape on all scales. In living organisms they are parts that have the same shape as the whole with smaller units structurally supporting larger units. God created a world using fractals with smaller immature organisms structurally supporting more mature organism at each stage of development. We know that early in the development if something goes wrong then that defect is continued in each stage of the development. What might be a small defect in the early stage of development may be profound in the mature organism. – Transformative Church Planting Movement*

Below are two triangles made up of small triangles or fractals. While they both look the same, they have developed in much different ways. The first starts with outside boundaries or the large triangle and creates smaller triangles within it while the second starts with one small triangle that reproduces and builds others on it. Most man-made structures are built the first way. Builders start with the shell made up of the foundation, walls, and roof and then build the inner rooms, such as the living room, kitchen, dining room, bedrooms, and bathrooms. In contrast, most God-made organisms, outside of the original creation of God, start with individual, small units, cells, or fractals that develop and reproduce to create larger, mature units. This is why a child early in development resembles an adult or a seedling resembles an adult plant. While the first way focuses on the outside of the structure, the second focuses on the infrastructure. This illustrates two different ways to build a church. While one focuses on the big unit or structure and then fills it with individual units, the other starts with individual units and develops them to a level of healthy reproduction, building the large unit. I call the first model the attractional model and the second model the natural model.

Before you think I am criticizing the attractional model, allow me to say that this is the model that reached me for Christ. My parents, who were both raised in the church, were attracted by a church that offered Vacation Bible School for their children, and although they did not attend church at that time, they sent me and my sister to VBS. It was there that I first heard the Gospel, which I later responded to. My surrender to Christ during VBS prompted the pastor to come to my house to talk to my parents about my need for baptism and their need to be in church. As a result, my mother joined the church, and my father came to know Christ and was later baptized. Today my 92-year-old father and 84-year-old mother, both in failing health, hate to miss a Sunday morning church service. Again, remember VBS was an attractional event created through advertising and promotion. In addition, throughout my life I have responded to attractional events. There were times that I had wandered away, and revivals and other attractional events brought me back. It was in one of these events that I surrendered to the ministry. Promise Keepers and The Harvest Crusades produced by Greg Laurie were pivotal in my development personally as a Christian and developmentally as a minister and church leader. I myself have successfully used this model to plant churches and renew existing ones. *Build it and they will come, plan and promote it and they will attend it,* and *expand your organization and then fill it* were driving motifs in my ministry, and they worked. Although I have not reached the world or grown a mega church, God has used me with some degree of success to start and renew churches.

A few years ago, I started a church with a lot of resources, in a young neighborhood filled with families. Along with a good core group, I had extra money, a nice building with a gym to play in, great contemporary worship, good relevant preaching, and seeker-sensitive outreach events such as sports camps and block parties. I did all the things that had worked in the past but this time had little results. I built it, planned and promoted it, and expanded my organization but without nearly the success of the past. The good news is I was not the only one. In my ministry area at that time, which included several churches, only two were really growing and only one was growing with lost people. My conclusion is this: I believe the days of an attractional church are numbered while the days of the natural church are coming. What attracted my parents and my generation, who had some connection to the church, will not effectively reach a generation that has no connection to any church. While my parents and I would never think of spiritual things without thinking of church, the present generation, whether you call it postmodern or pagan, can and does think of spiritual things without ever thinking of church.

> ...we live in a world where there is no clear religious majority, where individual belief in anything is popular, sincerity as the measure of truth is preferred, and moral relativity is predominant.

For many years, we have ridden the wave of being a "Christian nation," and when people spoke of God, it was the God of a Judeo-Christian society. After World War II, the attractional church with its Christian Crusades and revival campaigns tapped into this vein with great success among my father's generation of builders and with moderate success among my generation of boomers. Then again, in the latter portion of the 20th century when the boomers came of age, the attractional church reclaimed many of them with seeker-sensitivity, conservative Christian politics, the use of modern technology, and contemporary music. With all the gains of the church, however, it did not transform the culture, and Judeo-Christian influences became more and more in the minority. Although it would be distracting to the purposes of this book to go much further, suffice it to say that we live in a world where there is no clear religious majority, where individual belief in anything is popular, sincerity as the measure of truth is preferred, and moral relativity is predominant.

So, what is the church to do? The answer is simple. For many years I have said that all the issues of any church could be solved if that church would just do the Great Commission motivated by the Great Commandment. Now, I know this is not true. The truth is that all the world's issues could be solved if the individuals of the church would do the Great Commission motivated by the Great Commandment. Isn't it true that if the individuals in your church loved the people in their work place, home place, and play place, it would solve your church's problems and transform your community? Making disciples from the motive of love was the heartbeat of Jesus and the first century church, but not only did Jesus tell us to make disciples, He also told us how to do it. How do we make disciples? We go, baptize, and teach.

Jesus started it all when He left heaven (Go) (Philippians 2) to come to earth, baptized

His followers, and taught them to go. This was the first generation and formed the model for all Christians to follow. Again, in Acts, the Spirit came from heaven (Go) and filled the hearts of the believers, who responded to His work by sharing the Gospel (with 3000 believers being baptized). Through the Apostles in the temple and small groups in homes, these believers engaged the teachings of Jesus that transformed them and prepared them to Go. Go to baptize, baptize to teach, and teach to go was the model that was followed throughout Acts. We see the practice and results of it at Pentecost (Act 2), Samaria (Acts 8), Cornelius' house (Acts 10), Antioch (Acts 11), and the churches started by Paul. Although it is not itemized in every event of Acts, this process, established and commanded by Jesus, permeated the start, rise, and movement of the church described and outlined by Jesus in Acts 1:8—from Jerusalem to the uttermost parts of the world.

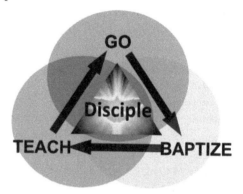

What is important to note at this point is that The Great Commission of Jesus is an issue of personal responsibility (small fractal) that permeates and describes the group or the church's obligation (large fractal). Churches should be disciple-making communities because the individuals in them are making disciples, and their leaders should be proven disciple-makers and disciple-making producers. The transformative culture's following or copying this simple, original model of go to baptize, baptize to teach, and teach to go helps preserve and maintain growth with integrity through multiple generations of believers.

Moreover, doing what Jesus told us to do, i.e., make disciples, in the way He told us and modeled for us by going, baptizing and teaching, does not start with the group. It starts with the one. Jesus, when He commissioned and sent the 12 and then the 70, did not tell them to find a group but to GO and find the ONE, the person of peace (Luke) or the worthy person (Matthew). In starting with the one made receptive by the Spirit of God, who becomes a follower, learner, and influencer, and in training him or her to go to baptize, baptize to teach, and teach to go, a first generation is formed. As we engage this first generation's God-given sphere of influence to find persons of peace, and as they become followers of Jesus expressed in baptism, we teach them to obey His teaching, transforming and making them Christ-like influencers. As influencers for Christ, we train them to go and baptize, making followers of Jesus. A second generation is launched. Making followers, learners, and influencers who go to baptize, baptize to teach, and teach to go forms the basic fractal of a transformative culture.

This fractal is not only the method; it is the measurement of success, ensuring reproduction with integrity at each level. It helps ensure that every generation is growing and healthy enough for reproduction. I once had a young man in my office to whom I had exposed this basic fractal. As we talked, I could tell he was reluctant to leave the small group in their church and venture out to do something new. It was a group of young marrieds with small children that he and his wife had been attending for two years. As he described it, I could tell it was a good group of individuals meeting together to study the Word, fellowship, and meet one another's needs. This was the ideal small group doing all that the church expected of them. It described many of the small group ministries today. Sounds good, right? Well, maybe not. I took a sheet of paper and drew the basic fractal—go to baptize, baptize to teach, and teach to go—and asked him, "When is the last time your group sent someone out to start a new group or ministry?" He responded, "Never." So I asked him a second question, "When has someone come into your group as a lost person or new Christian?" "Well, never," he answered. "So what do you do in your group?" As we concluded our conversation, it was this basic fractal that helped him see that his small group was more of a container than a conduit. Any individual, group, or church that studies the Bible and fellowships for an extended period of time without members coming in as a result of going or members going out as a result of teaching is not healthy. Doing only part of the fractal is unhealthy, and if the group does reproduce, often the result of conflict, it may pass on a defect to the next generation.

I did not create this fractal for measuring the success of ministry, from the individual, to individuals meeting one on one, to small groups, and to the church as a whole. It is **Jesus'** measurement of success. Jesus modeled this when He came from heaven to baptize His followers, taught them, and sent them to baptize. It interesting how quickly Jesus did things such as baptizing, teaching, and healing, both to and with His disciples, and then empowered them to do the same. According to John, Jesus, after baptizing His disciples, gave them the responsibility for baptizing others (John 4:1–2).

In a transformative culture, individual as followers of, learners of, and influencers for Jesus will, like Jesus, go to baptize, baptize to teach, and teach to go. Thus, when these individuals meet one-on-one in small groups and gather as the church, the fractal continues to be their measurement for success. Go to baptize, baptize to teach, and teach to go permeates the existence of a transformative church culture.

# CHAPTER 30: SIMPLE STRUCTURE TO ORGANIZE THINGS

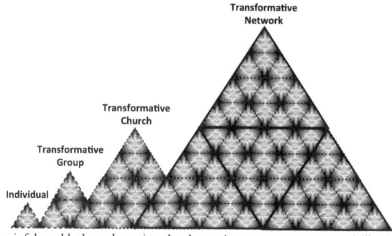

In a sinful world, the only option that humanity can use to preserve civilization and social order is legalism. Abuse, manipulation, greed, and resulting wrongdoing can be dealt with only by legislation that prohibits actions and a judicial system to enforce and adjudicate. All of this is designed to (hopefully) bring change to individuals from the outside in as they suffer the consequences of their wrongdoing and, thus, preserve freedom and order. The problem is that seldom does it ever change individuals who are caught by the system, and it continually complicates and often inhibits the freedoms of everyone else. Most of us would admit that we are often shackled by laws created to stop and punish others.

God's answer to the problems of humanity is much simpler – *I will put my law in their minds and write it on their hearts. I will be their God, and they will be my people Jeremiah 31:33 (NIV).* Instead of a moral code on the outside to govern the behaviors of society, God's desire is a moral code within each individual that will govern attitudes and then behaviors. Once again, we see that God's way is simple, individual, and based on the original (God writing on the heart of each person). The transformative culture is one where the structures focus on individuals using transformative groups, churches, and networks for accountability, encouragement, support, ministry, and missions. It begins with individual responsibility before it moves to group responsibility.

In much of this chapter, I will refer with little commentary to the descriptions and responsibilities presented in Chapter 12 of *Transformative Church Planting Movement*. I do this because I feel that they concisely state what each level of structure looks like and adequately describes who is in charge.

## TRANSFORMATIVE INDIVIDUALS

Start with one. One is the first. Without the first, there cannot be a second. Without the second, there cannot be the third. If this is true, then one is important. This is not the way we are used to doing church, but it is the way that Jesus did it and the way He told His disciples to do it. Start with the one: the person of peace.

One is the pattern for more. I have always told my first-born that he was practice for us. Parenting him created in us a pattern for parenting my other two. By pattern, I do not mean something that cannot be changed. Patterns can be adapted for different situations and circumstances, but they are nice to start with.

One is God's testing ground for many. God tells us to be faithful with the little and He will give us more. In all my years of ministry, I have noticed that the *appearance* of transformation in the church is easy to see in the group but difficult to see in individuals. When I am around other Christians, it is easy to be and/or act like a Christian. Like Peter among the other disciples, we are quick to profess, "I will never deny," but when we get all alone in front of the fire, things change—we change and what we said we would die for, we deny we ever knew. While group dynamics can be useful to bring about change, they can also be deceptive. Statistically, a significant number of young people from strong church youth groups drop out of church once they start college. These youth that served together, witnessed together, went on mission trips together, ministered to others together, and studied the Bible together somehow do not study, minister, serve, and witness alone. While you can have a semi-effective transformational group without all the individuals being transformed, you can never have transformed individuals that when they get together will not form a transformative group.

## TRANSFORMATIVE GENDER BASED GROUPS

*Transformative groups are the most powerful transformational environment. This safe, secure environment is where fellowship is stronger, nurturing is more intense, and individuals are held to the greatest level of accountability. Being gender specific allows for more sensitive topics to be addressed as they are exposed by God's Word. The size of the group needs to allow for significant sharing of the individuals in a reasonable time frame; therefore, a maximum of 6 individuals is suggested. The more people in a group, the more chance of losing the quiet individuals and the more time needed for everyone to share what God is teaching them. Individuals in the group are responsible for reading the assigned or agreed upon passages for the week and using the transformative process to share God's teaching to them.*

*One facilitator is needed for a transformative group. His or her role is to allow everyone to share what God is teaching them, and he or she is the spiritual guide of the group, always sensitive to the Holy Spirit's work in the lives of individuals and their need for prayer and accountability. The facilitator must be adept at using the transformative process, moving from feeding fish to teaching them how to fish for themselves. More and more, as they meet, the burden of transformation (knowing, seeing, feeling, doing, and being) is placed on the individual. The facilitator is always evaluating the group by the basic fractal, moving them toward going to baptize. Thus, his job is not just to facilitate but also to discover, develop, and help deploy new facilitators to create new transformative groups. – Transformative Church Planting Movement.*

This is the critical level between individuals and churches. It is a major missing component of transformation in churches today. It is gender-based because of the topics that will be revealed by the Holy Spirit and the Word of God. It allows men to talk about men things and women to talk about women things. Men need to talk about lust in the way that they lust while women need to talk about lust in the way that they lust. Men will share things with other men that they would never share in mixed company, and women do the same.

Each group should be small enough so that everyone shares in a reasonable time. This means that if someone is not talking, the group may be too large. You cannot hide in a transformative group. You are there to learn, share what you have learned, and be held accountable for what you have learned. Remember it starts with one. Do not wait until you have a certain number to start. Be faithful in the little, and God will give you more.

Every week, as you meet, it is all about the truth, the whole truth, and nothing but truth. It is a place for honesty (the truth) and openness (the whole or voluntary truth). Transformation can happen only when we are surrendered to the illumination of God's truth that comes through His Word.

As transformation takes place, individuals should be encouraged to pass it on. "Who do you know that would benefit from a group like this?" is a question that should be asked regularly. The Gospel or Good News it not just reserved for initial salvation; there should be ongoing stories of sanctification. It is Good News when God saves me from the penalty of sin, and it is Good News when He saves me from the power of sin. When God does His Good News work of daily transformation, we must be ready to share this Gospel or Good News with others. I have never known anyone who had to go through a twelve-week course to know how to share good news he or she has experienced. Like falling in love, the birth of a child, or getting a new job, good news is easy and natural to share.

## TRANSFORMATIVE CHURCHES

*The Transformative Church is where multiple transformative groups gather weekly in homes or other places to discuss what God is teaching them through their individual reading and transformative group experiences. In the Transformative Church, a meal is shared, the Lord's Supper is taken, the Word is presented, and transformational work in the individual is discussed and witnessed by the group. Leadership exists to guide and facilitate, not to teach and force application. Individuals are responsible for bringing God's transformative work in their life to the group for encouragement, ministry, prayer, and/or accountability. Again, the size of the group is conducive to allow for significant sharing of the individuals in a reasonable time frame; a suggested maximum is twenty people.*

*Another aspect of the Transformative Church is that it thinks generationally beyond the family to the extended family. The Transformative Church does not exist to get bigger; it exists to reproduce. It is always in a state of change because it is continually moving people through the process of being followers of, learners of, and influencers for Christ. The church then births influencers into new communities who make disciples and start again. The church will also be in a state of change because people that are unwilling to surrender totally to the process of becoming influencers and taking responsibility for their own spiritual growth may at some point stop attending. After much grace and a great deal of patience and tolerance, the Transformative Church is always prepared to let go of the unreceptive who at any level may choose to stop developing. As Jesus said, at times you must "shake the dust off your feet" and move on to those who are moving with God (Matthew 10:14).*

*Every Transformative Church will need at least three leaders: a Pastor/Facilitator Leader, a Ministry*

*Leader, and a Missional Leader. The Pastor/Leader/Facilitator is the chief leader of the church and the facilitator of the weekly church gatherings that center on the Transformative Word with a goal of teach to go. He is responsible for the Transformative Group Facilitators, and they are responsible to him. Working with the Ministry and Missional Leaders, he will discover, develop, and deploy Transformative Group Facilitators. Ministry Leaders are responsible for developing transformative relationships with a goal of baptize to teach. This leader keeps the church focused on the needs of the group. He or she works with the pastor to create new transformative groups. The Mission Leader is responsible for helping people discover their transformative calling with a goal of go to baptize. He or she also keeps the groups focused on missional opportunities including local, regional, national, and international (Acts 1:8). These three working leaders, with the Transformative Network Leader, will discover, develop, and deploy leadership for new churches. – Transformative Church Planting Movement*

In a transformative culture these groups form the ministry and missional arms. They are empowered to do the work of the church. They teach the word, care for people, reach out into their communities, and start new groups and churches. Integrity is ensured because these churches are always launched with three leaders described above whose focus on different aspects keeps the group Biblical, pastoral, missional and reproductive, which correlate with the basic fractal of disciple-making: go to baptize, baptize to teach and teach to go.

## TRANSFORMATIVE NETWORKS

*A Transformative Network supports and resources the churches; it does not exist to develop programs, campaigns, or slogans for them. It exists to resource them and work with them to help train new leaders and launch new churches and transformative groups. Networks may meet monthly or weekly in events that may look like a traditional church with worship and the proclamation of God's word. They may even through gatherings or other events produce entry points to a relationship with Christ, but they will always move people into participation in transformative churches and transformative groups.*

*A network will have at least one Network Leader to help with and administrate the ministries of a network. Often he is the core church planter who started the TCPM and raised up the first generation of leaders. He is the leader of leaders, the father of the local movement. Continuing to lead by example, he is the facilitator of a group and church. – Transformative Church Planting Movement*

The transformative culture is made up of a network of churches and church leaders. Elders of the network are the pastors and leaders of the churches who have earned authority, not positional authority. These leaders understand the pulse of their churches and bring this wisdom to the network meeting and the network leader. These leaders form the guiding counsel for the churches of their network under the direction and service of the network leader. Moreover, in my present ministry, this level forms the job description for potential church planters. I am not looking for the man who can gather a crowd—I am looking for one who can make disciples and disciple-makers and who can organize and lead the network as a movement of God. In other words, he is also expected to create a network where success is measured by an ability to go to baptize, baptize to teach, and teach to go.

# CHAPTER 32: SIMPLE SYSTEM FOR ACCOUNTABILITY

Accountability is an important part of a transformative culture. To maintain the integrity of the culture, each believer in every generation must have a healthy accountability system. I call this system an accountability wheel. Just like the pressure in a tire must be maintained for it to roll properly, every individual must have all the components in the accountability wheel to maintain healthy spiritual development that makes up a healthy transformative environment.

## DAVID AND NATHAN

*2 Samuel 12:1-15 (NIV) David burned with anger against the man and said to Nathan, "As surely as the LORD lives, the man who did this deserves to die! He must pay for that lamb four times over, because he did such a thing and had no pity." Then Nathan said to David, "You are the man! This is what the LORD, the God of Israel, says: 'I anointed you king over Israel, and I delivered you from the hand of Saul. I gave your master's house to you, and your master's wives into your arms. I gave you the house of Israel and Judah. And if all this had been too little, I would have given you even more.'"*

It begins with you. No! It begins with a spiritually healthy you! One thing you must have to be a spiritually healthy Christian is accountability. You must surround yourself with people who love you enough to speak the truth, people who love and encourage you, and people in whose lives you are actively encouraging and speaking the truth.

David, the man after God's heart, forgot his need for accountability at the pinnacle of his success. With no one empowered to ask him the hard questions, he becomes arrogant, commits adultery and murder, and initiates a cover-up. In the passage above, we see David having successfully hidden his sin from the world. Not only has he hidden it, but he has also used it to his political advantage. He is now seen as the king who has taken the widow of one of his fallen soldiers into his home to care for her. "Oh, how King David loves and cares for his men" is the talk of the town. All is well or well-hidden until God sends Nathan to expose David's treachery.

> *...who have you empowered to ask you the hard questions about your time, talents, and resources?*

Nathan tells David a story that would appeal to the little shepherd boy within him. David probably remembered having lambs in his flock that were more pets than livestock. As David hears about the story of a man who feeds his guest the pet lamb stolen from his neighbor's fold, he becomes furious. Nathan the wise prophet, at the climax of David's rage, points his bony finger at David's face and says, "You are the man!" He then supports his case for David being the cruel neighbor in the story in spite of all the blessings God had bestowed upon David. *Anointed King, delivered from the hand of Saul, given the house and kingdom of Saul* are part of the list proving David's sin against grace. The final nail in Nathan's argument of accusation, and this must have been the proverbial straw, had to be: *if all this had been too little, I would have given you even more.*

What went wrong? Where did he make the wrong turn to head down such a perverted road? The answer is that David failed to allow others to speak into his life. What if in the beginning of his lustful fancies, David had empowered Nathan, who could have asked him, "Why do you go to the roof at night? What are you looking at?" He may even have confronted him with, "Stop! Think about what you are doing!" Wouldn't it have been better if David had had someone who could have said, "David don't be that man" instead of "David, you are the man!" Every preacher or leader who has fallen into sin and public disgrace has followed this same pattern. They have removed or lost all the friends who could critique their decision making.

The question is: whom have you empowered to ask you the hard questions about your time, talents, and resources? Who asks you about your unaccounted for money and time? To whom have you given the right to do what Nathan did to David? Who has the right regarding your sin to say, "You are the man. You are responsible"? Who can ask you the hard questions such as, "What are you doing with your time? What are you doing with your money? What are you doing with your talents? What are you doing with your soul or life?"

If you never hold yourself accountable, sooner or later God will. Consider the following.

*Romans 3:19 (NIV) Now we know that whatever the law says, it says to those who are under the law, so that every mouth may be silenced and the whole world held accountable to God.*

*Romans 14:9-12 (NIV) For we will all stand before God's judgment seat. It is written:" 'As surely as I live,' says the Lord, 'every knee will bow before me; every tongue will confess to God.'" So then, each of us will give an account of himself to God.*

*2 Corinthians 5:10 (NIV) For we must all appear before the judgment seat of Christ, that each one may receive what is due him for the things done while in the body, whether good or bad.*

## ACCOUNTABILITY IS ABOUT AUTHORITY

Authority is the issue. If you say God is sovereign, the ruler of all things and the ruler of your life, you must surrender to His authority and the spiritual authority HE has placed in your life. You cannot be surrendered to God without being surrendered to the people God has placed in your life.

In addition, this authority is an issue of honor, not just obedience. While obedience to authority can be forced, honor is always a choice. I could make my children clean up their rooms, but I could not make them like it or me. Biblical accountability is about obedience from a heart of honor or about honor that leads to obedience.

## PARTS OF THE ACCOUNTABILITY WHEEL

A healthy accountability system has three types of people in two layers of accountability. Types of accountability include Pauls who are empowering people, Barnabases who are encouraging people, and Timothys who are followers. You need these types of individuals in two levels or layers. Invasive people are those you have a personal relationship with who empower, encourage, and follow you. They know you and can do surgery on your soul or you can do surgery on theirs. Non-invasive are people who empower, encourage, or follow you but with whom you do not have a personal relationship.

### *What does a Paul look like?*

A Paul is a leader you have chosen to follow—a person who influences, empowers and/or inspires you. He may be a model to emulate, a mentor, or a coach. He is a person you trust who has journeyed ahead of you in different areas of life. Examples may be pastors, advisors, inspirational writers, counselors, coaches, or sponsors. An invasive Paul would be a person who knows and can comment on the good, bad, and ugly of your life—your strengths and especially your weaknesses. He is a person who, when he disagrees with you, tears you up and drives you to your knees. When you feel this person is disappointed in you, it hurts. A non-invasive Paul would be a person or people who empower and challenge you from a distance, such as favorite authors, preachers, and teachers. You know them, but they do not know you from Adam.

*Hebrews 13:17 (NIV) Obey your leaders and submit to their authority. They keep watch over you as men who must give an account. Obey them so that their work will be a joy, not a burden, for that would be of no advantage to you.*

### *What does a Barnabas look like?*

Barnabas means "Son of Encouragement." This is the person who encourages and supports you, who empathetically relates to you. An example may be a co-worker, friend, or support group member. An invasive Barnabas would be one who relates and comforts you personally while a non-invasive person does the same without personally knowing you.

*Proverbs 27:17 (NIV) As iron sharpens iron, so one man sharpens another.*

*Ecclesiastes 4:9-12 (NIV) Two are better than one, because they have a good return for their work:* [10]*If one falls down, his friend can help him up. But pity the man who falls and has no one to help him up!* [11]*Also, if two lie down together, they will keep warm. But how can one keep warm alone?* [12]*Though one may be overpowered, two can defend themselves. A cord of three strands is not quickly broken.*

### *What does a Timothy look like?*

A Timothy is a person you influence, inspire, and empower. It is someone to whom you convey knowledge and/or wisdom—a person who respects and desires your opinions and advice and sees you as an example or model to follow. Examples of this may include students, younger or inexperienced friends, or an apprentice. An invasive Timothy would be the person who has given you permission to dialogue with them on a personal level while a non-invasive one would be the person that you empower but have no personal contact with, such as a person who reads your blogs or other writings. Most accountability in this area is chosen from the bottom up, not the top down. While you can choose your Pauls and Barnabases, Timothys must choose to surrender to your guidance.

One of the best illustrations of healthy accountability is a comparison between the Sea of Galilee and the Dead Sea. While the Sea of Galilee is teeming with life, the Dead Sea is not. The reason is that the Sea of Galilee has a healthy flow of water in and out—in from the surrounding mountains and out through the Jordan River. The Dead Sea, on the other hand, receives water from the Jordan River, but this water escapes only by evaporation, leaving a stagnant body of water filled with minerals and unable to sustain life. God created and saved us to be more like the Sea of Galilee than the Dead Sea, more like a conduit than a container. All that God gives and allows in our lives is for the purpose of raising us up to send us out—for us and then others. The world is starving for the Bread of Life; thus, we should be one beggar telling another beggar where The Bread is. According to the passages below, the comforted should comfort, the reconciled should reconcile, and the taught should teach.

*2 Corinthians 1:3-4 (NIV) Praise be to the God and Father of our Lord Jesus Christ, the Father of compassion and the God of all comfort, 4who comforts us in all our troubles, so that we can comfort those in any trouble with the comfort we ourselves receive from God.*

*2 Corinthians 5:17-21 (NIV) Therefore, if anyone is in Christ, the new creation has come: The old has gone, the new is here! 18 All this is from God, who reconciled us to himself through Christ and gave us the ministry of reconciliation: 19 that God was reconciling the world to himself in Christ, not counting people's sins against them. And he has committed to us the message of reconciliation. 20 We are therefore Christ's ambassadors, as though God were making his appeal through us. We implore you on Christ's behalf: Be reconciled to God. 21 God made him who had no sin to be sin for us, so that in him we might become the righteousness of God.*

*2 Timothy 2:1-2 (NIV) You then, my son, be strong in the grace that is in Christ Jesus. 2 And the things you have heard me say in the presence of many witnesses entrust to reliable people who will also be qualified to teach others.*

## FLAT SPOTS

As a tire needs air pressure to stay inflated, healthy accountability needs individuals of each type and at both levels: invasive and noninvasive. If one area is lacking, it produces a flat spot. These flats spots are places where we are weak and may become susceptible to sin and a loss of integrity. For example, not having any Pauls in my life may lead to arrogance and the problems of David. Like David, if we have not empowered people to speak into our lives and to ask us the hard questions about what we are doing with our time, talents, and treasures, then gifts from God may become viewed as entitlements. A lack of Timothys may be a recipe for becoming a spoiled Christian with everything coming in and nothing going out. We absorb all the church can give without passing any of it on. Like spoiled teenagers, we want all the privileges but none of the responsibilities. Just like becoming a parent has a way of growing spoiled children into responsible adults, taking on a Timothy may be the critical step in the development of a Christian. Not only do we need people in front of us to guide us and behind us to follow us, we need people beside us to support us. Not having Barnabases in one's life will lead to burnout and a lack of productivity. Like Moses needed

Aaron and Hur to hold up his arms so that Joshua could lead Israel to victory, we need someone to hold our arms up as we lead and help others.

Growth with integrity is maintained in part when every believer in every generation develops a healthy accountability system. The accountability system flows naturally through each part of the transformative structure, from one-on-one discipleship, to gender based groups, and to a church (small group). Because it permeates this cellular level, the culture maintains growth with integrity.

# CHAPTER 33: APPLICATION TO EXISTING CHURCHES

I have asked many pastors of existing churches if they would rather have a church full of followers or a church full of leaders, and, thus far without exception, they have told me they would rather have a church full of leaders. Like them, most of us would like to preach to people on Sunday who are turning their world upside down for Christ Monday through Saturday. We would all like to be equippers of the saints to do the work of the ministry. Instead, many pastors are the only ones doing the work of ministry in and outside their churches.

The ideas in this book work best in a highly decentralized structure that is started from scratch. While it may be difficult to implement them in an existing church, it would not be impossible.

## OPTION 1: REPURPOSE, RETRAIN, AND EMPOWER WHAT YOU'VE GOT

Most churches have in place similar designs and structures. They have small groups and small group leaders. They often have formal or informal gender-based mentoring relationships for helping individuals. Finally, these churches offer Sunday church where individuals and groups get together. If a church were strategic and intentional, it could retrain mentors to function as transformative group leaders, it could repurpose, retrain, and empower small groups to be ministry centers, and it could utilize Sunday mornings to set the stage for transformative Bible studies. Perhaps the church could even be retrained to be highly reproductive units under the leadership of staff.

## OPTION 2: CREATE NEW WINESKINS FOR NEW WINE

Although repurposing is one way, a better way may be to create a new track with new training. Utilizing and adapting the ideas in this book, an existing church could create a new track of transformative gender-based groups and transformative small groups that could be described as new wineskins for new wine. This new track could run alongside the old track, allowing people to move into it as the Spirit leads and they become ready.

# APPENDIX: TRANSFORMATIVE PROCESS QUESTIONS

## PRELIMINARY QUESTIONS:
- Did you read the passage? How many times?
- What questions do you have about this passage?
- What bugs you about what you read?

## KNOWLEDGE
- What are the facts? Tell me the story.
- Who is speaking?
- What questions are being asked? What are the answers being offered?
- What is the response of others the information given in this passage?
- Who are they speaking to?
- What are they speaking about?
- What is being said?
- What is being done?
- What is the context of this passage?
- What is the story as you understand it?

## PERSPECTIVE
- What do you see beyond the facts?
- What impressed you about the passage? Why?
- Who do you identify with in this passage? Why?
- What does this passage say about God? …about you? …about others? …about all three?
- What do you see as the most important part of this passage? Why?
- What does this passage mean to you?
- What do you think God is saying to you through this passage?

## CONVICTION
- How do you think they felt?
- What happens if we do not obey? How do you feel about it?
- What feelings are being conveyed in this passage?
- How do you think the speaker felt? …hearer?
- What truth emotionally grabs you attention? How does it I make you feel?
- How do you feel about the people in the story?
- Is there anything in this passage that makes you…
  - …angry?
  - …happy?
  - …sad?
  - ….guilty?
  - …hopeful?
  - …thankful?
  - …uncomfortable

## COMPETENCE
- What truth do you need to do something about?
- How can I pray for you?
- In light of the passage, what changes do you need to make?
- In light of this passage, what will you do different?
- In the light of this passage, do you need to… …forgive someone? …seek forgiveness?
- What do you need to pray about concerning this passage?

- How can we pray for you in regards to this passage?
- What is your greatest obstacle to fulfilling this command?
- What do I need to pray about in regards to this passage?
- How can God help you? What do you need to pray about?
- How can we hold you accountable?

## Transformational Competence Helps: GET SPECIFIC with God's Word. Is there…

…**Glory** to acknowledge? Is there an exaltation that needs to be given to God? Something to praise God for?

…**Error** to avoid? Examination to be taken? Test to be passed? Is there any problem that I should be alert to or be aware of?

…**Thanks** to be given? Is there something here I can be thankful for?

…**Sin** to confess? Do I need to make any restitution?

…**Promise** to claim? Is it a universal promise? Have I met the condition(s)?

…**Example** to follow? Is it a positive example for me to copy or a negative one to avoid?

…**Command** to obey? Am I willing to do it no matter how I feel?

…**Idea** to challenge? Attitude to change? Am I willing to work on a negative attitude and begin building toward a positive one?

…**Fact** to trust? Truth to believe? What new things can I learn about God the Father, Jesus Christ, the Holy Spirit, or the other biblical teachings?

…**Intention** to analyze? Motives to be examined?

…**Conduct** to be incorporated? Is there an application that needs to be applied?

## Character

- How will this change you?
- How will doing this make you more like Jesus?
- What do you see as the outcome of living this way?
- What is your desired result from this truth?

## The Great Commandment: Read Matthew 22: 37-40

### Preliminary Questions:

- Did you read the passage? How many times?
- What questions do you have about this passage?
- What bugs you about what you read?

### Knowledge:

- What is the story?
- What is the context of Jesus' teaching?
- Why does give this teaching?
- What is being said?

### Perspective:

- What does it say about God? …me? ….others?
- What is the meaning of love to you?
- What would the world be like if it functioned like this?
- What does this tell you about Christianity and being a follower of Christ?

- What does this tell me about God's expectation of man?
- In light of this being a command, what does it say about Christianity?
- Conviction:
- How do you feel about what this commandment says about being a Christian?
- In light of these expectation, how do you feel you measure up?
- How does that make you feel?
- How do you think the man who asked the question felt about Jesus' answer?
- How do you feel about it?
- What happens if we do not obey? How do you feel about this?
- Is there anything in this passage that makes you…
    - …angry?
    - …happy?
    - …sad?
    - ….guilty?
    - …hopeful?
    - …thankful?
    - …uncomfortable?

## COMPETENCE:
- How will you love God this way this week?
- How would you love others as yourself?
- How would you love God with all your heart soul and mind?
- What do you need to pray about concerning this passage?
- How can we pray for you in regards to this passage?
- What is your greatest obstacle to fulfilling this command?
- What do I need to pray about in regards to this passage?
- How can God help you? What do you need to pray about?
- How can we hold you accountable?

## CHARACTER
- How will this change you?
- How will doing this make you more like Jesus?
- What do you see as the outcome of living this way?
- What is your desired result from this truth?

# THE GREAT COMMISSION: READ MATTHEW 28:18-22

## KNOWLEDGE:
- What is the context of the passage?
- Who is speaking and to whom are they speaking?
- What does Jesus say?

## PERSPECTIVE
- What does the passage tell you about Jesus?
- What does say about others?
- What does it say to you and me?
- What does it mean to make a disciple?
- If Go baptize and teach are the process of making a disciple,
- What does "Go" mean to you?
- What does "baptizing" mean to you?
- What does "teaching to obey" mean to you?

- Where do I see myself in this process?
- What happen if we do not obey this teaching?

## CONVICTION:
- What impresses you about this passage? Why?
- How do you feel about this commandment from Jesus?
- What happen if we do not obey this teaching? How do you feel about this?
- Is there anything in this passage that makes you...
  - ...angry?
  - ...happy?
  - ...sad?
  - ....guilty?
  - ...hopeful?
  - ...thankful?
  - ...uncomfortable?

## COMPETENCE:
- What do you need to do about this passage?
- What behaviors do you need to in cooperate in order to obey this command?
- What is your greatest obstacle to fulfilling this command
- What do I need to pray about in regards to this passage?
- How can God help you? What do you need to pray about?
- How can we pray for you?
- How can we hold you accountable?

## CHARACTER
- How will this change you?
- How will doing this make you more like Jesus?
- What do you see as the outcome of living this way?
- What is your desired result from this truth?

# EPHESIANS 2:1-10

## PRELIMINARY QUESTIONS:
- Did you read the passage? How many times?
- What questions do you have about this passage?
- What bugs you about what you read?

## KNOWLEDGE
- What does is Paul saying?
- Who is he talking to?
- What seems to be the theme of these verses?
- What topics are being addressed?

## PERSPECTIVE:
- What words or phrases stand out to you? Why?
- What does this say about God? ...you? ...others?
- What do you think is most important in the passage?
- What impressed you about this passage?
- What do you think others need to know?

## CONVICTION:
- What feelings do you get from reading this passage?
- What do you feel God is saying to you?
- How do you feel about the phrase…
    - … (v1) you were dead in your transgressions and sins?
    - … (v3) children of wrath?
    - … (v5) made us alive with Christ?
    - … (v5) it is by grace you have been saved?
    - … (v6) And God raised us up with Christ?
    - … (v6) seated us with Him in the heavenly realms in Christ Jesus?
- Is there anything in this passage that makes you…
    - …angry?
    - …happy?
    - …sad?
    - ….guilty?
    - …hopeful?
    - …thankful?
    - …uncomfortable?

## COMPETENCE
- What needs to change in your life in light of what you read?
- What truths have gained that need action immediately? What is the action?
- What do I need to pray about in regards to this passage?
- How can God help you? What do you need to pray about?
- How can we pray for you?
- How can we hold you accountable?

## CHARACTER
- How will this change you?
- How will doing this make you more like Jesus?
- What do you see as the outcome of living this way?
- What is your desired result from this truth